HELP
DON'T HINDER
DRIVER COACHING – THE SECRET BIBLE

MARK SHAUN RITCHIE

You can help too

As a coach I have dedicated my career to helping thousands of people, and through this publication, will help thousands more. Not only will it help further pupils, parents and driving instructors, but by purchasing this book you will be donating a portion of the proceeds to the BRAKE and EAAA charities. You'll be helping these two amazing causes, which in turn could help you or a family member in a time of need.

Here's an insight into who they are and what they do.

YOU CAN HELP TOO

T: 01484 559909
www.brake.org.uk

There are five people killed every day on UK roads and hundreds more seriously injured. Brake is a national road safety charity dedicated to preventing road deaths and injuries, as well as supporting people bereaved and injured in road crashes. Every road death is a tragedy. Every road death is preventable. At Brake, we believe that safe and healthy mobility is everyone's human right and we're working to make that right a reality.

If you feel you are in a position to assist and would like yourself personally or your business to help, please contact: 01484 559909 to find out how, or visit www.brake.org.uk

Ben Walker
Community Fundraiser

M: 07894 475020
E: ben.walker@eaaa.org.uk
www.eaaa.org.uk

The East Anglian Air Ambulance exists to save lives by delivering highly skilled doctors and critical care paramedics by air or car to seriously ill or injured people in the region. We are a life-saving charity covering Bedfordshire, Cambridgeshire, Norfolk and Suffolk that is only kept airborne thanks to our incredible supporters. Since the charity's launch in 2000, we have attended over 25,000 life-saving missions and are tasked an average of eight times a day across our two bases in Norwich and Cambridge. We receive no regular government funding and rely almost entirely on public donations.

There is currently a seven-hour gap in our service between midnight and 7am where no helicopter air ambulance is available to the people of East Anglia. We are campaigning to become a 24/7 service by 2020 at an additional cost of £1m a year and need the public's help to raise the funds.

Find out more and support our mission online:
www.mission247.co.uk

HELP – DON'T HINDER

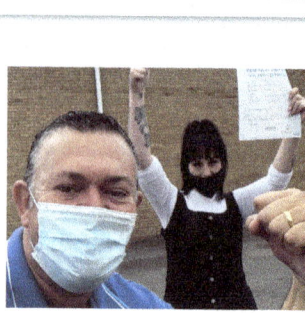 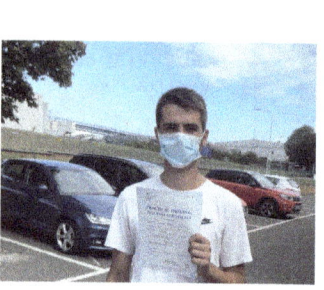 

CONTENTS

Introduction 7

Reasons for this Book 11

Client-Centred Learning 19

The Lessons 22

The Manoeuvres 24

Techniques and Faults 38

Giving up Your Right to Drive 54

The Theory Test 63

The Test 69

Funny Stories 89

With Grateful Thanks 94

Acknowledgements 103

This book is designed as a training aid to help alongside driving tuition. It is not intended to replace any other publications and the training suggested is of my personal opinions and methodology only.

INTRODUCTION

HELP – DON'T HINDER

Introduction

Hello. My name is Mark Ritchie, a successful driving instructor with over two decades of experience. I am self-employed and a father of two wonderful children. Driving has been my life ever since I can remember and after passing my test at 17 years old I bought my first car, which gave me great freedom, independence, a choice of jobs and girlfriends.

I joined Her Majesty's Forces for a great 5 years as a Royal Pioneer infantry soldier, but was unfortunately medically discharged due to a very serious back injury.

It was here where I first discovered I had a passion to teach driving as I received a resettlement course off the armed forces and was soon granted a Provisional Driving Instructors licence. I was given a small partnership in Bungay (Suffolk) with the opportunity of buying the business if I qualified, it was a great goal to go for at the very young age of 22, I would have probably been the youngest instructor in the UK.

Unfortunately things didn't go right for me, I could never pass the exams the DVSA had set, but still I knew how to teach and get fantastic results, because my pupils all passed, but I could never understand what the examiners where looking for from me. However, I chose never to quit, I loved the job, meeting new people working my own hours around the restrictions and limitations of my disability, seeing my pupils faces when they passed, knowing how much it meant to them and being part of their life, seeing them blossom from complete novices to drivers of great ability, that was my reward.

Naturally the income helped as well and was an inspiration to carry on.

To qualify as a DVSA instructor you are required to pass parts 1, 2 and 3 tests. If you fail part 3 you may only take the test 2 more times and then, if you've failed your 3rd test, you have a 2 year wait before being allowed to retry.

Most people who get into this predicament have no choice but to go and find a new career and live happily ever after, well that's the theory.

I, on the other hand, invested into the public house trade with my friend who was already the tenant, only to find the business wasn't doing what it should have, and I lost everything. As this happened I was approached by someone who had seen the enthusiasm and efforts I'd made and advised me there was a vacancy on the other side of town. Three days later I was the new manager of a members sports and social club which I must say was once again a business on its last legs before I got there.

INTRODUCTION

After the bad times of fights and heartache, with being broken into and threatened with protection rackets and whatever else, I decided to call it a day.

Then, as this was the last weekend of trading, I received the devastating news that my older brother had passed away. Very sad times.

Thereafter I failed my ADI test another 3 times, and found myself back on the 2-year waiting list.

INSPIRATION

In-between jobs I kept teaching myself and refreshing my tuition skills, I never stopped. A few months later I married for a very short period and soon found it wasn't working out.

But during this relationship, the opportunity arose to become a hackney carriage driver. I enjoyed the work and the company that I was sub contracted to and did this until I met the real love of my life. We had plans to get married and I had another go for my ADI badge as the money in taxis was getting harder to come by. Shortly after that test, I had another go, to no avail.

Now being married and having spent a fortune on weddings for the second-time round, I found myself entangled with gambling, going to the casinos, playing from the bookies or even the television to raise money for my new family's future. I then had great delight in hearing that I was an expectant father.

This was fantastic news and I was completely overjoyed, but I was badly addicted to gambling and not doing well.

Naturally my wife and I exchanged words and she was a rock bigger than Everest for me.

This was probably the first time I had a mind shift, something inside me shone through, I had a thought: I wanted to change, I made a decision, at that exact moment in time CHANGE already took place, I never looked back at gambling again as I knew now the stakes were too high, not the money, but my family and their love.

I asked myself 2 questions.

> 1) **What am I doing to improve my income RIGHT now?** I looked a bit dumb struck and then question number 2 entered my mind.
>
> 2) **How much money am I planning to be worth at 65?** Still dumb struck. I never thought about it. Who does, right? We just get on with life day by day, we don't question it, we just do it. We find a place in life, our comfort zone and play it safe, hopefully the world will leave us alone and that's it.

So, I sat down and thought hard about it, why my life had been this hard. First I blamed my injury: Look at me now being DISABLED…I can't do what I want to do… Why should I bother? I won't ever can be the best I can be now… Leading to depression.

I won't ever be able to live the way and in the manner I would like to live, or have the things I want, see the things and places I want to see.

INTRODUCTION

Once a big optimist, I was now a pessimist (look at how many negative thoughts I had just being disabled, not to mention everything else I blamed...)

I carefully realised that perhaps I had the wrong attitude; I was using excuses for MY LIFE. I had developed over a short time from being out of the forces bad RITUALS. Regular bad decisions which in turn became a crisis. I was always complaining, THINKING ALWAYS ON NEGATIVE ENERGY.

So apart from my injury, losing my job and various other factors in life, what was the difference in my mindset before I joined the forces when life was great to where I was after my troubles... The only answer was "my mind"

Recognising I could change my thoughts on gambling instantly, perhaps I wasn't too late to change my attitude, my rituals, my thinking... Perhaps, I said, my brain is not disabled. Let's have a go. So I said to myself, yes, life hits you, and it can hit you hard, but it isn't how hard you get hit, it's how you get up and keep moving forward, going that extra round.

Here is an interesting formula, a LAW if you like: Our rewards in life will always be in exact proportion to our contribution or service. Put another way: The money you are paid is in direct proportion to the NEED and your ABILITY and the degree of TROUBLE in replacing you.

Now I happen to believe everyone on this planet is self-made, we've all had the same tools when born, we all have a mind, a consciousness and sub-consciousness, the freedom to think, the freedom to have ideas, to be creative. Today people have access to vast amounts of knowledge, education and information, some CHOOSE to use it, some CHOOSE not to.

But everyone has CHOICE.

The way we think determines ourselves, life in the outside world is a mirror image of our inside world.

Work hard on ourselves, feed our brains with good ingredients by reading more and creating positive energy and learn how to control all the negative thoughts and your inner self will, without exception, be enriched, thus projecting a better you to the outside world.

I had one chance left now on my driving instructors course to pass this wretched exam. In debt up to my eyeballs, a baby on the way... No pressure.

And then I passed, I finally passed, with comments like "a fantastic attitude", "great use of the verbal commands", "excellent ability to instruct", all the things I needed to hear, all at the right time.

I know that overwhelming feeling of success and sense of achievement and still see these today, I share this emotion with each one of my pupils today through their eyes.

And fully understand how they feel when very occasionally things don't go as planned.

After spending all these times learning different techniques on how to deliver the training, from all over the country, with different mentors and different points of views, having time to reflect on my own performance, very useful tips and guidance from other instructors and examiners over the last 24 years, I now believe I can give open and honest information to aid any person wishing to learn the art of driving on today's roads and traffic.

REASONS FOR THIS BOOK

HELP – DON'T HINDER

Reasons for this book

After instructing driving tuition for 20+ years I have seen huge changes in the way tests are being examined, in the pupil's learning ability and readiness for today's roads, the pupil's attitude, their way of thinking and the cost of lessons, tests and all other areas of financial strain on the family's resources.

Many parents try to advise their children or family members on how to teach and the way they were told 30 years ago, and these mentors believe, hand on heart, they must be right. Naturally these actions may confuse the best of children as mums and dads are never wrong and should not be challenged!

Pupils delicately, sometimes query the instructor's ability, until the instructor gives a perfect explanation of the situation, giving the reasons and answers the pupil can accept and understand, and can then go back to their parents chuffed and proud that they know something that mum and dad don't!

As parents, we don't want to show signs of weakness or embarrassment and therefore shrug it off, but may reflect later and quietly think oops! Which normally means that the parents don't then quickly get involved in the future, if this sounds like you, please keep reading.

Instructors like mum and dad's input, the more the merrier, because broadening knowledge can only be a good thing. It generates a great opportunity for family involvement, which, let's be honest, when children are aged between 15 – 25 years they want their own independence, and family interaction is sometimes lost. Often the sad thing is this probably is the most important time in their life, when family interaction is desperately needed.

I believe I can help from my own meandering experiences, how to give you an input on your child's life and driving, after all we all went to parent's meetings throughout their schooling, and yet parents are backing off now when their child is about to take their 1st real test in the 'adult world' environment in which sadly you may have a limited involvement, and for no real reason.

Some parents leave tuition completely with their chosen instructor, some parents train the pupil themselves, as far as they can, and other children don't get the opportunity at all. I strongly believe everybody should be able to drive, and could drive, and enjoy the flexibility of driving and reaping the rewards i.e. more choice on the career front, etc.

I believe driving is a privilege and not a matter of a right.

I want to not only share with you a fully illustrated step by step guide on how to drive, but also how I deliver all those awkward areas of training. I also wish to explain to you as parents, what the Examiners would like to see, how to achieve these goals. How to interact with your chosen instructor in a positive manner, for an accelerated learning curve for your child (which ultimately will save you money for them or on their behalf).

REASONS FOR THIS BOOK

To inform you of the use of language Examiners and Instructors use (getting to know the lingo) but also for those parents that wish to teach their own child themselves for their own reason and be successful 1st time in test conditions, but more importantly be safe on our roads today.

Hopefully it won't be just your family's member that learns modern driving techniques, I hope it's the whole of your family that gains knowledge and confidence in many different aspects.

With this book, it is also suitable for self-teaching, many pupils who have self-taught have normally, in my experience lived out in the sticks, miles away from any town where tests take place, and would have needed a good 4 to 5 hour lesson just to get into the town.

The cost implications were far too high on a weekly basis for them.

One of the other primary concerns for 'older drivers' is to know when to give up their keys. Normally after the age of 70 you have to reapply for your licence, which requires filling in a DVLA form asking about medical conditions. Successful drivers may find that family members make observations and constructive criticisms to encourage the driver to hand in their keys, and sometimes there's tough love, whereby the driver does not have much say and the family intervene for the greater good. If you find you are the driver in any of these situations, then perhaps this book will make things obvious to you, or prepare you for when that time comes and you will understand the reasons for family concern.

I personally teach a 60 plus course. This is a voluntary course suitable for any driver over the age of 60 or anyone who hasn't driven for a number of years and lacks confidence, and is anxious to find out first hand if they have cause for concern, to enrich their current driving technique, bearing in mind that they were taught 40 or maybe 60 years previously and even though they have evolved naturally there may well be new rules still to be passed on. Their new car may be an automatic as opposed to the traditional type. The course I run is very like the government's Pass Plus course, adapting some of the modules slightly to benefit the driver's needs.

HOW WILL THIS BOOK HELP ME?
- Teaching my offspring or family members to drive.
- Teaching myself to drive.
- Refreshing myself to drive.
- Understanding what the Driving Standards Agency requires for the test of practical ability.
- Recognising terminology used by Instructors and Examiners.
- Knowing when to give up my keys.
- How to interact with Instructors.
- How I would choose an Instructor.
- What other courses are available to broaden my knowledge?
- Training the mindset to produce positivity and confidence.
- How to deliver the training in a suitable way for awesome results.
- Leading by example.

REASONS FOR THIS BOOK

Okay let's start with a lesson plan. We need a structure in place: the pupil needs to know what he will be doing for the next few hours. The fact you have told them what you will be covering will start them thinking about this subject right away, any knowledge they possess they will naturally want to share with you! They want to please! With their enthusiasm, I think this will get them in the right frame of mind before you start.

Secondly, making the lesson for a set time is also important. The 1st reason for this is if you finish the subject and start a new subject the pupil will feel a huge sense of achievement, in their mind they have done more than what was expected from them, they are making progress! By applying yourself to my lesson plan and structure below the situation of not being able to complete your aims for the lesson causing arguments or disappointments shouldn't arise. However, I will come back to this situation in my trouble shooting brief further into this book.

THE STRUCTURE

- Recap of the last lesson (ask some open questions on the last lesson) listen carefully to their verbal answer, if it's wrong pick them up on it, but praise them for trying and keep them encouraged.
- Aim of today's lesson.
- Briefing of the aim and the goals you would like to achieve (but be realistic). I will lay out the structure I use for average pupil's ability from my own years of experience for you, naturally if the pupil has shown great ability for practical learning, or is below average, you can tweak this structure to suit their individual needs.
- Delivering the information is vital, make sure you know the subject otherwise the info will come across confusing and potentially disastrous as questions will be asked and you cannot have a lack of confidence in your answer, they are looking up to you, and you can end up getting side tracked and the quality of the lesson will change and so will their enthusiasm. Naturally questions should always be asked, don't be scared of saying "I'm not sure" as long as you also say "I will look into that and get back to you" and make sure you do! Then this also helps build up trust and care that they need from you.
- Practise... Get them driving, start your lesson. You have explained what they are to do in the briefing, you have given them opportunity to ask them any questions now let them explore this.
- Make sure you have taken them to an area that is relevant for the lesson.
- Make them feel relaxed and at ease, crack a joke or two before you start, but keep control of them, when they make mistakes which they will, talk to them, explain and identify what the fault was, analyse the fault, ask them why they might think that fault happened, tell them what effect this action or fault could do and then give them the remedial action, i.e. how we can put it right, and get them to repeat their previous action, and talk them through it so they can build their confidence up, and repeat again but giving less information, until they show sound knowledge (perhaps the fault they caused today could be used in a question in the next lesson, when doing the recap on today's lesson!) It could save making the same mistakes each week if the pupil is mindful of it before they

REASONS FOR THIS BOOK

start the lesson. So, feel free to make your own notes, it's certainly good for conversation at the end of the lesson when you have a debrief.

- Debrief – allocate a good 10-15 minutes to have a good debrief. Discuss weak areas first and interact with the pupil to let them tell you how they would put it right. Once again keep it light, very little pressure 'it doesn't matter, we got there in the end' approach. Then discuss all the good points, think praise wherever possible, so they are feeling on a high, and then close your brief with "Look forward to the next lesson when we are going to…" Having them on side awaiting the next time you go out is fantastic for learning, this also gives you the chance to talk on a one to one.

- With the pupil, if it's a family member, this could be a good way to communicate with them building up your relationship with them, as there are fewer distractions in a car that's parked, than they might find at home!

- Make sure you have the legal-sized L plates on the driver's side of the car, front and rear.

- Have a rear view mirror for your use (these can be purchased for a very modest fee).

- Always have 2 pens and paper for notes and diagrams to help explain situations. You can even buy colour presenters on line which includes prompts and training aids that are laid out effectively.

- Instruct as early as possible, it takes time for the pupil to absorb information and apply the thought process and leave time for a corrective action, after all PREVENTION is far better than the cure, so don't rush them. If possible, they will gain speed naturally as they get used to the procedure and up their confidence.

Now let's look at a structure, learning to drive is very much like a jigsaw puzzle, it's easy for us as we know the complete picture but to the pupil there are 5,000 unfamiliar pieces in front of them, so the structure is vital, breaking down this mountain of information that you are bursting to get across into bite size pieces, in a logical way. For the average pupil, I would have laid out 15 lesson plans, this equates to 15 weeks at 2 hours a week, totalling 30 hours (national average is approximately 44 hours) however this is because not all pupils or instructors are the same.

LESSON STRUCTURE

Lesson 1 - Controls lesson.
Lesson 2 - Moving off and stopping.
Lesson 3 - The use of mirrors, and signals.
Lesson 4 - Turning left and right, from major to minor roads.
Lesson 5 - T-junctions.
Lesson 6 - Cross roads.
Lesson 7 - Roundabouts and emergency stops.
Lesson 8 - Pedestrian crossings and use of signals.
Lesson 9 - Hazard perception and meeting traffic.

REASONS FOR THIS BOOK

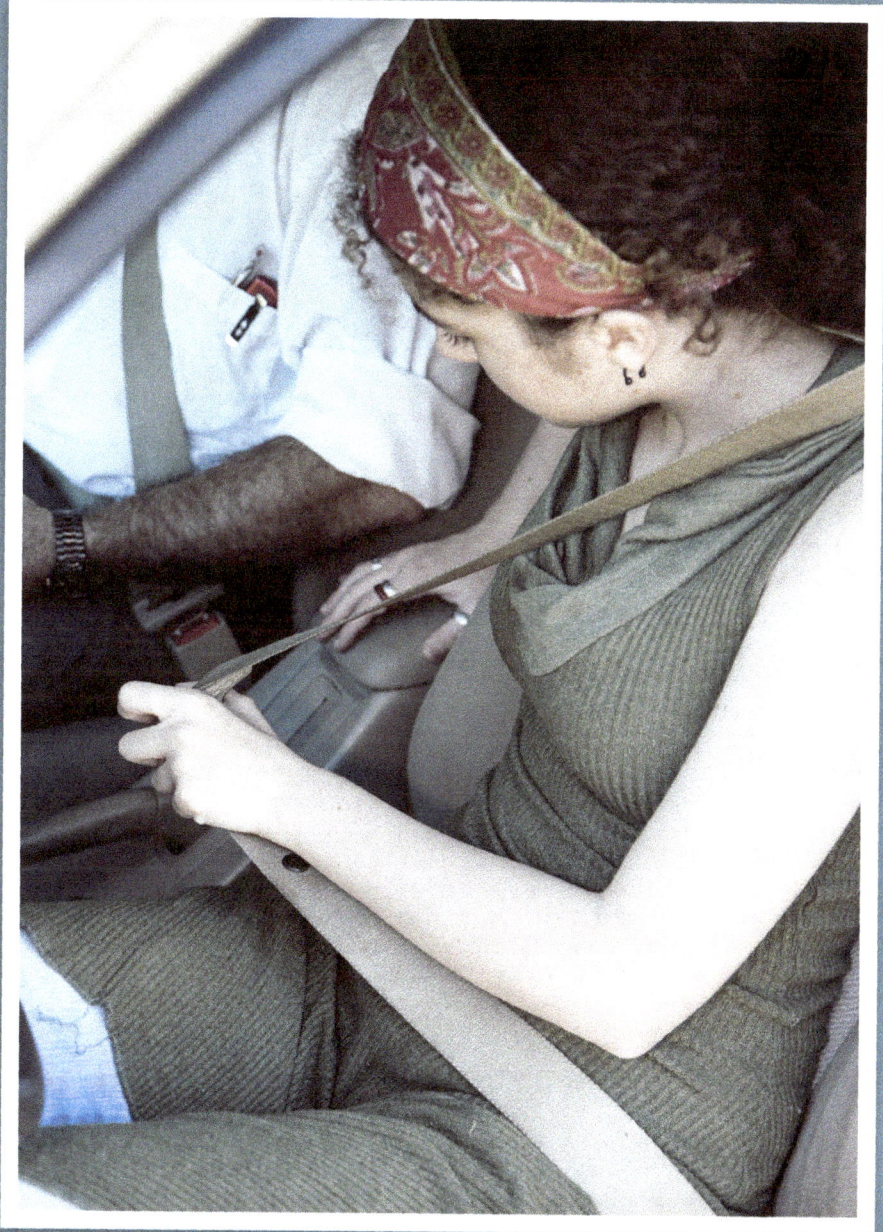

HELP – DON'T HINDER

REASONS FOR THIS BOOK

Now, I personally think that if the pupil has got to this stage, around the 18 hours lesson time frame of road sense, then we need to change the teaching side to more of a 'question and answer' technique. (Transferring responsibility). You should naturally see from the work you have done with them, that they have already picked up a good driving ability, and you would have noticed that you don't need to keep repeating instructions. If however you are, then try really hard to back off a bit, as they won't learn much themselves and may become too reliant on you, instead of thinking for themselves and you wouldn't have done them any favours, so ask them questions that are relevant to the moment. This will prompt their memory and their thinking. I think to myself if they haven't acted on something by the time I would have, then they need prompting or telling outright which you must do as they learn quicker from success than failure.

Lesson 10 - Turn in the road using forward and reverse gears.
Lesson 11 - Reversing around left corner / sharp and sweeping.
Lesson 12 - Parallel Park.
Lesson 13 - Dual carriageways.
Lesson 14 - Bay parking.
Lesson 15 - Pull up on the right.
Lesson 16 - Mock test (look at faults, practise areas of weakness, then another mock test and continue again and again if required).

You may well find you can cover two lessons in one session i.e. 'emergency stop' and 'pedestrian crossings' or 'T-Junctions' and 'crossroads' etc... bonus. In the past I have managed to achieve three manoeuvres in a 2-hour lesson where at the end of that lesson their manoeuvres were at test standard!

As you can appreciate there are many ways to pass your knowledge on, that's why every driving school is different, why every instructor is different. Word of mouth is great for recommending instructors, but don't shoot your friend if you find the instructor is no good for you, and it does not mean the instructor is rubbish! I like to think of myself as a good all-rounder, using different techniques to match the pupil's requirements, gaining knowledge of various topics to help build a great rapport with the individuals I **coach**. Know I have just highlighted the word "coach" because since I have become an instructor I have evolved with the times and found coaching is by far the best ART and tool there is for pupils to gain the knowledge they need, another name for this is "client-centred learning". This becomes an art because it takes time and practice with this tool to make it effective, but boy when you get it right, the results are stupendous.

So, you might think, what's the difference between an **Instructor** and a **Coach**? Well to me an Instructor "instructs" he explains or shows. Sometimes this is great and sometimes desperately needed, whereas a "coach" gets the pupil to answer by asking a series of questions.

So, you are probably asking yourself right now, I'm paying this person money to train me, why isn't he telling me? Why is he asking me? The answer is so simple; your goal is to be able to pass the dreaded test! His aim is for you to pass the test, and having the ability to **drive safely for the rest of your life.**

We all went to school, we all listened to what our dear teachers said, we all took the same exam, but we didn't all get the same results.

The people that got higher grades either maintained information better or repeated the work again and again until they generally understood it. Because the outside information was passed on from one to another, information either got rejected, misconstrued, lost, which is why civilization now in its 3rd millennium has only progressed this far, yet look what's happened over the last 30 years, mobile phones, computers, technology, jobs, degrees, weapons, etc. We are now understanding the importance of how to share the knowledge.

> So, when it comes to driving, look how I could teach the same subject and watch what happens:
> - This is a steering wheel, it turns the car left and right, you need to change the amount of steering depending on how fast you are going and the severity of the bend.
> - What's this? (Pupil: it's the steering wheel). What does it do? (Pupil: It steers the car which way you want to go). Do you need to steer it lots or a little at a time? (Pupil: Well I think small amounts so I don't over steer but can always add more if I wish or need). How did you know that? (Pupil: I see my mum and dad drive and they always do this).

Out of the two situations which method do you think the pupils learn from best? Hopefully you would agree with the second. But look closer, I'm involving the pupil, getting the pupil to interact with me, the pupil is demonstrating he/she understands, because they told me so!

The pupil's confidence is gaining, they got a question right! Your opportunity to praise them has been created, opening more opportunity to ask further questions, for example: What's the danger of over steering? (Pupil: Well I could hit the kerb, or end up in the wrong place on the road). What's the danger with this then? (Pupil: Well I could burst a tyre or run over a pedestrian, or even be in the line of oncoming traffic). So if you were turning to your right when should you take your steering off? As you are straight or just before you are straight? (Hmmm… Well I need time to take the steering off so just before I'm straight?). That's fantastic!! Let's go and practice.

You can clearly see the advantage all round how "coaching or client-centred learning" makes a huge difference. Then the 'instructor side' can come in by explaining tips or methods to fine tune! But you extracted the information from the pupil, so it cheats the intellectual immune systems but gets the results of long term memory and putting the pupil in the best position possible which is the natural ability, getting the pupil to make their own decisions based on the knowledge and skills they already possess. We as instructors purely chisel away barriers or blocks and carve the pupil into whatever the pupil wishes to do! In this case drive the car to a very high level giving them the tools to do this continuously, whilst promoting or curving their attitude in the process to be an ambassador to all other road users, by setting great examples of road craft for other motorists to learn from.

Now let's look a lot closer at individual lessons.

CLIENT-CENTRED LEARNING

HELP – DON'T HINDER

Client-centred learning

One of the best techniques I use daily is CCL otherwise known as client-centred learning, this means finding the answer from within. Sounds mysterious, well it's overlooked and not exercised enough in today's world and to be brutally honest, it's very hard to master – so what exactly is this path of tuition?

When I explained in my book about how fast your mind is able to make a conscious decision in a nano second, well this goes hand in hand like machine learning, putting the information into a zip file somewhere in your mind to recall that data or a similar at a moment's notice. Now imagine we have an intellectual immune system, our immune system itself doesn't know what's right or wrong. You see, if we are poorly, our immune system finds the cause and attacks it! Killing diseases or infections is what we employ it to do! But what if you needed a life changing transplant, once we have the perfect match and transplant is all done to save your life and suddenly your body rejects it, the immune system is saying it's not ours … go away.. and does exactly what it is designed to do… remove foreign bodies, etc… Now in your mind, you also have an intellectual immune system (here I could talk and talk and talk) but that information gets lost, misunderstood, twisted, because it's coming from a foreign source. How many times has someone said "Hey, can I have a brew with 2 sugars and milk" and 10 seconds later you find yourself forgetting what they said, and having to go back and ask? Happens to me a lot, due to distractions all around us. We spend hours of our life learning how to get distracted, so you can imagine the frustration caused to the pupil and to the instructor on multiple tasks that need action immediately, after all, driving is one of those life skills that require serious multitasking functions. So a way to beat this intellectual immune system is, I ask the pupil what they think, provoking thoughts, why do you think this? How do you think this would happen, etc…

So for example me saying to a pupil, when should you check your mirrors? And why? The answer I expect back would be: to see what's behind or the side of me and as often as possible. Okay, but the answer they gave doesn't really have much substance, the pupil hasn't really made a direct link from the unknown to the known, so I follow with more questions like: what might you be about to do, whilst travelling at 30mph, where you need to use your rear view mirror? The mind then processes this and they may turn round and say "oh the rear view mirror sees behind and if I'm doing 30mph I could be about to brake that would be important to see what's behind me, and the following natural thought would be: depending on how close or far the following traffic is behind me will dictate how hard I should brake!" Right… So the pupil has now told me when and why they should check the mirror, they have a link and then I can explore this further by saying "Okay, so apart from slowing down, when else?" After a second or 2 the pupil would say: speeding up! "I would ask why? They would then think and recognise the immediate danger of speeding up when something could be overtaking them!

So the conclusion is they have physically told me when they would use it, why they would use it and how they would use it, linking the unknown to the newly learnt known, all coming from inside them! No foreign thoughts, thus beating the intellectual immune system! And they have learnt it for life. Far, far better than

HELP – DON'T HINDER

CLIENT-CENTRED LEARNING

me spending lessons saying check your mirrors every five minutes. Now the reason I've piped up about CCL is because so many people put driving off until it becomes essential in their lives.

If I received £1 from each pupil saying "I know nothing", "I'm useless", "I haven't a clue", "I'm scared" etc, I'd be a retired millionaire by now!

In this book I have talked about fear and why pupils hold themselves back, sabotaging their chances of starting or finishing for that matter, but I want to draw your focus away from putting things off any further, especially if your thoughts are focused on "I know nothing" or "I'm too daft".

I did an experiment during the Covid lockdown in May 2020 to confirm my thought process, I asked a 12 year old boy, at random with no training or knowledge apart from his own experience of what he has seen or believe to be right with no prompting or outside help whatsoever! I asked him if he could send me a picture – drawn on a computer if he likes, as that's what 12 year olds enjoy doing – of:

1) A parallel park
2) Emergency stop
3) Reverse around a left corner
4) Foot pedals driver side – and asked him to write any information in that he felt was helpful to someone else!
5) Bay park

This is what I received back:

So he recognised you drive on the left, he said keep both hands on the wheel and brake firmly, assessing the situation as quickly as you can! Well that sums it up about right!

Bay parking, okay so not much detail here but he knows what bays are and is facing the right way! To be fair if I said steer left or right he would end up in a bay or reversed and steered he wouldn't be a million miles off!

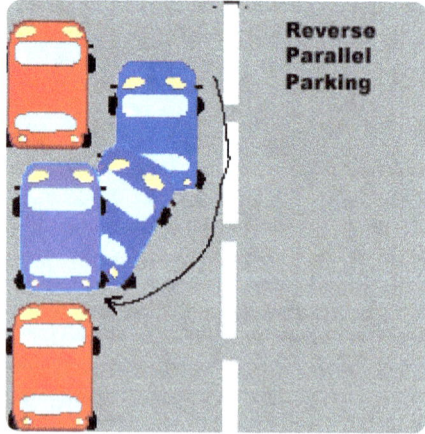

So he has shown great knowledge of what it is, the aim of what he wants to do and position for finishing! Remember he is only 12 years old with no lessons!

And here a reverse around the corner, he understands major road and minor road, he knows his objectives and has a clear vision on how to achieve this task.

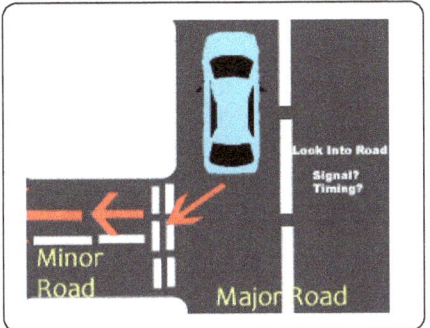

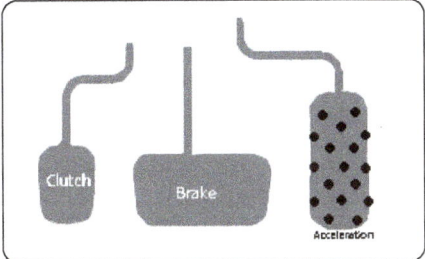

100% correct,

Now the picture of a steering wheel, doesn't seem much, however once again he knows what it is and he has it the right way up!

I would like to take this opportunity to say a massive thank you to Theo Kells for producing these very fine pieces of graphic design and thank you Theo for joining in on my experiment, you have just proved that 5 years before you are allowed to drive – and being 5 years younger than most of the learner drivers around the rest of the world – that you have a great understanding of multiple areas of driving.

Deep down I believe everybody has something to contribute, you don't know nothing, you know something! You've been around for at least 17 years with your eyes open so despite your limited belief in yourself, have some optimism that your chosen instructor that uses CCL will extract information from yourself which in turn should boost your confidence beyond your initial thoughts!

(Note CCL is Client Centred Learning, otherwise known as Student or Pupil Centred Learning).

THE LESSONS

The Lessons

Firstly, do some preparation work, make sure your car is set up nicely for them, L plates and mirrors in the correct position, no rubbish under the seats that could hinder seat adjustment or get in the way of their feet whilst driving, make sure the radio is off and you have enough fuel!

Is your pupil adequately insured and is the car roadworthy? We must also think about route planning. For the first lesson it is normally a good idea to take them somewhere quiet, not too much traffic or any hazards – a long straight road is usually good. Thereafter try to plan routes that will be useful for that lesson, trying to fit in the area that will be reintroduced in the next lesson, so they have half an idea on what they can expect. If you go off course don't worry, use all roads as training aids as it's not just the roads they are learning, it's the traffic situation that changes the dynamics of the roads we use!

People often say to me "Crumbs, don't you get fed up going round and round town, all day long, everyday?" My answer is quite simply, no, it's not the roads I see, it's the developing hazards that aren't the same. Every time something changes you have something to talk about or to quiz the pupil over, and even if they drive really well, you can bet your bottom dollar some other driver will make an error, so you have a great training aid right there. Use somebody else's misfortune for a discussion, you will never be able to cover all the scenarios on the roads but use as many as possible, get your pupil to try and anticipate the road ahead, ask them to always think 'what if?'. Get them to look at road markings, all signs and reading the road ahead!

If in the event, you don't have much local knowledge, have a look on web sites such as multimap.com etc, or street maps but whatever you do, don't go from easy routes straight to hard ones, remember when planning a route, they must be able to go back around a circuit to correct any errors and they are learning in small quantities, so the transition, easy to hard routes, should ideally be unnoticeable, otherwise you will knock their confidence or put them off.

If this is their 1st lesson, drive them to the chosen starting point, but talk to them on the way, they may well be nervous, so give them something to think about, perhaps explain your hand position on the wheel, why you hold the wheels at the 10 to 2 position, how firm to hold the wheel, how much steering is needed, demonstrate how to feed the wheel using the push pull method, explain why holding or steering the wheel incorrectly could cause problems, get them involved from the start.

Next we have the BRIEFING! Word of advice – keep the brief……BRIEF.

I always recap on the previous lesson using a question-and-answer technique, for example "Can you remember what we did last week?" "What mistakes did you make?" "How did we correct those errors?"

Always try to make your questions open, that is, in a way that they would need to explain the answer, not with a simple "yes" or "no". When starting my questions. I always try and remember to include "How," "when," " where," " what," and "why,"?" etc.

A few well directed questions on the previous lesson could well stop old faults arising, building confidence and generally making progress, if their verbal answer is wrong, that shows a gap or misunderstanding in their training, put it right, give them another briefing on that subject, by asking them relevant questions, it will soon be clear where the problem lies.

Praise them wherever you can, even if they only get it half right, at least they got half right! Keep their moral up, don't just say "wrong" …. "Nope" …. "Don't be thick" etc….. even if you feel like it! This will do nothing for them at all.

In this brief after recapping on the last lesson, go onto the 'AIM' of today's lesson, what you are going to do and what you are hoping to achieve, if it's going to be a manoeuvre then I suggest you get closer to the training area you have chosen, as whatever you have explained will soon be forgotten unless you are nearly ready to practise.

I would proceed with a full briefing, step by step of the manoeuvre, then get them to execute it in practise with a full talk through, as they do it, then again with perhaps just prompts in key areas, and this you may do jumping in verbally if they get stuck, then when you think they may be able to do this with no assistance at all, tell them "right you're on your own now, let's just see what you can do."

If they lash it up…. okay, do your fault analysis, which includes the real identification of faults, why the mistake happened and how to put it right (remedial action) and do the manoeuvre again.

If the manoeuvre, such as 'parking', was a success get them to get out of the car, let them see for themselves how good their efforts were. As I keep saying confidence builds confidence, and you can quite easily say "well hang on before you say you can't do this" it was only the other lesson when you couldn't do a manoeuvre but you saw your final result, it was brilliant, so come on let's have a go at this… in the event they ever become a little wobbly.

If it's not a manoeuvre your briefing was on, with your well-planned route for that lesson, then it shouldn't be too long before they practise what you have preached! However, be flexible as sometimes situations arise on the road which you need to deal with, and I hope you would use it as a training aid. I had a classic myself recently, I was ready to teach dual carriage ways only to find on the approach the dual carriageway was closed due to an accident, we got diverted to the countryside, so we pulled up and I gave a briefing on 'emergency stop' etc….. but still linked it into the dual carriage way. I wondered what caused the accident? How close were the other drivers travelling to each other? We covered lots of situations such as perhaps emerging traffic, overtaking, vehicle or driver error, adopting an accident avoidance technique, which naturally brought us to the 'Emergency stop' lesson, so lessons can go pear shaped but it's always worth having a backup plan! The quality of the lesson may not suffer at all if you are flexible to adapt quickly.

Most of my briefs are no longer than 8-10 minutes, I hate wasting valuable driving time, and most of the time pupils do too!

But use the coaching technique.

THE MANOEUVRES

The Manoeuvres

In tests today, the Examiners require the pupil to complete just one manoeuvre. At the Examiner's discretion, he will advise the pupil to pull over and park up normally giving more detail, such as "if you could park behind the red car" or "just before that road on your left" etc. so the pupil knows exactly where to stop.

Other times the examiner may well say "I would like you to pull over in a safe convenient and legal place please". On both occasions the examiner is looking for mirrors signal and manoeuvre routine however in the 2nd quote he is also assessing the pupil's ability to unaided look for a **safe place** i.e. not on a corner, too close to junctions, not obstructing moving traffic or becoming a hazard in any way, a **legal place**, not on double yellow lines or zigzag lines etc.....and **convenient place**, this could be things like bus stops or hard up against trees or walls etc. for example.

So, if you try this with the pupil then start off easy advise them to pull over giving them lots of notice so they have time to look, assess, decide and act, hopefully they end up parking where you wanted them too!

By giving them short notice like "pull up before that car" will not only test their strength of their mirrors and signal knowledge but also the control of the car including the steering, and always think if you could do it so should they, because that's the level they need to be at.

Any mistakes made should be discussed now and rectified, also try and get the pupil to think **why**? The reason for parking in the 1st place, look where you are, if it's behind another vehicle the examiner may wish for you to carry out a reverse parallel park, or an angle start,**(in the event that it is an angle start then ensure the pupil gives effective observation over their right shoulder before hand brake comes off, and at least a further two right shoulder checks as they move out, and wait till they have got their steering straight before increasing their speed, this will automatically prevent over-steering stresses!).**

If it's a wide road then perhaps a turn in the road using forward and reverse gears manoeuvre, or if it's before a road on the left it may be a reverse around a corner, etc.... so knowing this may help foresee what's going to happen next so they can start preparing themselves, there again the examiner may well want the pupil to just move off again safely and under control.

1 TURN IN THE ROAD USING FORWARD AND REVERSE GEARS

This manoeuvre was once known as "the three point turn" as roads became smaller the DSA (Driving Standards Agency) changed this to "turn in the road using forward and reverse gears", the logic behind this was simply with some roads it's really hard to successfully turn the vehicle around using only three points of contact without touching any kerbs under full control, so let's speak the same language as the examiners, you don't have to manoeuvre the vehicle round in three turns with tight roads, it can be in five or even seven points as long as the road requires it.

Naturally you will get marked down if it takes seven points and you could achieve it in three!

The reason for learning this manoeuvre is simply to turn the vehicle around to face the opposite direction, if there are no side roads to reverse into.

Common sense would suggest that you would not complete or even attempt this manoeuvre in a one-way street, near where bends prevail etc..... just remember you are the hazard don't make it more hazardous than it already is!

- Ensure car is in a great parking position, close to your kerb and straight.
- Put the car into 1st gear.
- All round observation starting with your left shoulder, consulting left exterior mirror, looking at the road ahead, right exterior mirror, at the same time finding your clutch biting point, and looking over your right shoulder to check your blind spot.
- As you bring your head back to face the front release your hand brake and move forward very slowly, showing good use of your clutch pedal under control edging the vehicle forward. (The reason why I like to take my hand brake off as I brought my head straight, is to minimize the possibility of anything coming from the direction I'm about to move into. **(Always look to 'the direction of travel' last.**
- Start steering as quickly as possible to your right, ensuring you feed the wheel using the **push pull method**, by keeping the vehicle slow should help with this. **(The best combination to turn the car around is to steer fast but keep car slow)**
- As you near the opposite kerb, try and steer to the left, getting as much 'steering lock' on as possible, some is better than none. **(Take into consideration the roads camber!)**
- Once you have got close to the kerb pause, you can (if you find you still have lots of room to move forward) try finding some sort of reference point, I suggest to my pupils that when it looks like my right exterior mirror looks like it's about to go over their kerb pause!) I find in my car this can be useful until they have a good knowledge of the size of the vehicle.

Continued over the page

THE MANOEUVRES

Continued from previous page

- Apply the hand brake.
- Now select reverse gear and find biting point.
- Look up and down the road, if any traffic is coming which your manoeuvre would affect, then stay paused until either the traffic has moved around you or until they have physically stopped to allow you to continue. **Remember there is no pressure on you**, if traffic has stopped then they are happy to wait! They are aware of what and why you are manoeuvring the car.
- If this is the case look again to confirm your original thoughts, then looking over your left shoulder out of your back window, release the handbrake, once you have full control of your biting point, reversing your car back slowly, continue steering to the left.
- As you reach half way across the road look over your right shoulder towards your new kerb. It is important to **look in the direction of travel.**
- Once again as you get close to the kerb start steering to the right as quickly as possible until you feel you can't proceed much further due to touching the kerb. (I use the British kite mark in the front driver's window, as that looks like it's about to mount the kerb, I pause, in my car its perfect, however you may find another reference point that suits you better).
- Apply the hand brake to secure your car again.
- Select 1st gear and find biting point.
- Once again look up and down the road and give traffic the opportunity to pass, and if all is clear then ensure your biting point is good whilst finishing your observations, and release the hand brake. **(think camber)**.
- With full control of your clutch, controlling your speed, using the push pull steering technique, continue your steering to the right, this steers the car in such a manor to be able to park in your normal parking position.
- Apply hand brake to secure your car and select neutral to show the Examiner you have completed this manoeuvre.

Please remember to look at the road you are doing this manoeuvre in, i.e. is it up hill, flat or down hill, is there a camber in the road **(camber is where the middle of the road is higher than the sides for drainage purposes)** as these will all dictate how much clutch or brake to use, practise all manoeuvres with different gradients wherever possible.

On the test the examiner looks for control and observations, you are not in a rush, and you are the hazard, pedestrians on a path in front or behind you are also classed as traffic so give way to them and make sure they are out of harm's way before you proceed.

THE MANOEUVRES

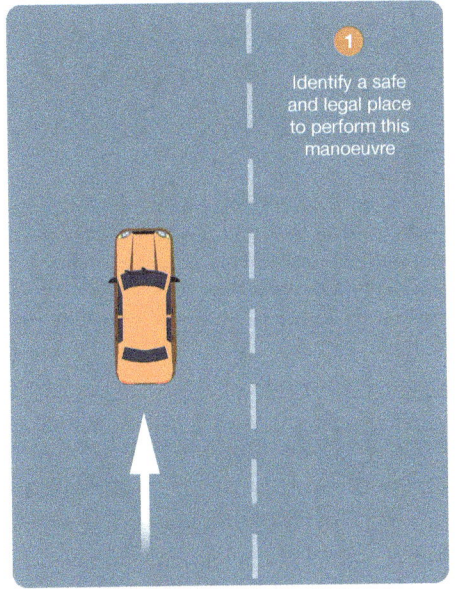

1. Identify a safe and legal place to perform this manoeuvre

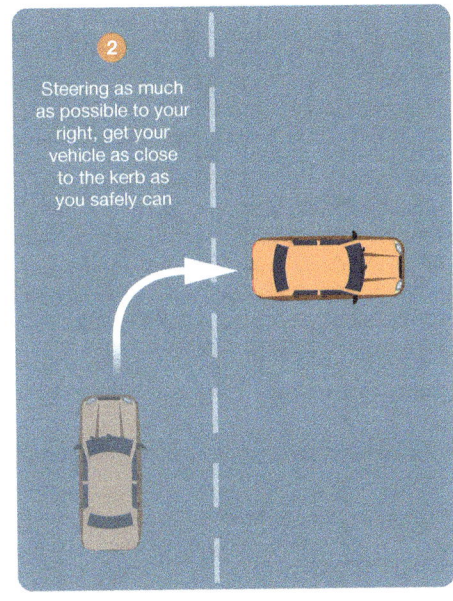

2. Steering as much as possible to your right, get your vehicle as close to the kerb as you safely can

3. Engage reverse gear and manoeuvre your vehicle back slowly, steering to the left

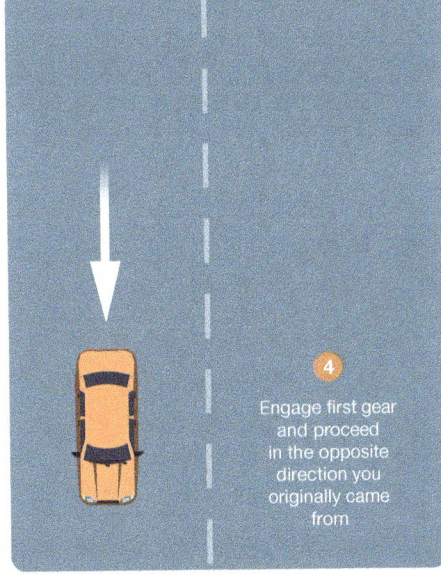

4. Engage first gear and proceed in the opposite direction you originally came from

HELP – DON'T HINDER

THE MANOEUVRES

 ## THE REVERSE AROUND THE CORNER (LEFT)

The reason for this manoeuvre is because, if in the event you have gone the wrong way you can turn the vehicle around without blocking the main road. The examiner will ask the pupil to pull over just before the next minor road on the left. (Minor road would be a side road and a major road being a main road).

Once parked in your normal parking position ensure you apply hand brake then neutral so he knows you have made the car secure and can listen. The examiner will go on to say "I would like you to pull past the next road on the left and reverse around the corner staying reasonably close to the kerb and under full control, and continue back about 3-4 car lengths, in your own time, please continue". So, on hearing the examiner asking you to pull over, try as always to find that safe, convenient and legal place, remembering to consult your main mirror 1st, followed by your direction mirror which should be in this case your left exterior mirror and considering a signal if required.

Sometimes there may not be a very suitable place to pull over so by all means suggest this as most of the time the examiner may over look this and will advise you to pull up anyway, no problem as they have asked you to, they will in no way deliberately set you up to fail you.

Then when starting off to begin this manoeuvre check your blind spot just before you move off and as you drive past the road you will reverse around look carefully at this road, ask yourself is it going uphill, downhill, any drains, or small bricks or rubbish etc....are there any vehicles or hazards in the road and what sort of bend is it, is the bend you are to reverse around sharp or sweeping?

If there is a vehicle approaching from behind then maximise your signal by indicating when you are half way past the minor road if possible and pull over 2-3 cars past the minor road, a good tip is to park a little bit wider than normal, as if you were to make a steering error you may have an opportunity to correct this error.

Once again once parked make the car secure, compose yourself and relax, you do have all the time in the world, select reverse gear, find biting point, give all round effective observation starting with the right shoulder as you want to look in the direction of travel last, and as you are looking over your left shoulder through the back window, release the hand brake. **(if you are going downhill then leave your clutch in and roll using your foot brake purely to control your speed. If reversing uphill ensure you do have your biting point as you do not want to roll forwards by mistake as this shows lack of control, serious fault!)**

As you reverse back remember you are the hazard so keep the car as slow as possible you need to observe around the car constantly, if any thing comes then pause, this shows 1) you have seen the traffic to the examiner, and 2) It is easier for traffic to assess and over take you if you're not moving.

If you are nearly in the minor road, then still pause. You are not in a hurry.

As you reverse back the minor road should disappear from the rear window and then reappear in the back passenger window, if the road has a sweeping kerb then may I suggest strongly that as the kerb is now entering passenger rear window steer quickly 1 complete turn to the left, as you come back you can either steer more or less for you to stay close to the kerb using your left exterior mirror, although most of your time should be spent looking behind you, make sure you check for any new traffic entering the road from the front (tip....as you look to the front check your left exterior mirror to confirm your position to the kerb and

THE MANOEUVRES

again on the way back from the observations from the front). By keeping the car moving slowly you will soon see the car lining up parallel to the kerb, take off the 1 left turn and then any adjustments to the steering can be made allowing a remedial action if a steering mistake was to be made.

Remember if you want to go closer to the kerb which should be to your left then steer to the left! When reversing always steer in the direction of which you want the back of the car to go.

As you become parallel to the kerb (gap of about 15-30 inch's) then continue approx. 3-4 car lengths back, checking for other traffic to the front regularly. The reason for coming back so far is purely to allow other vehicles to overtake and reposition before the T-junction.

Last of all, pause the car, apply the hand brake to secure the car and select neutral, so the examiner recognizes that you have finished.

Now if the corner is "sharp" then everything is the same as before, however when you can see the road you are reversing into becomes visible then keep coming back until the kerb looks like its approx. half way in the rear passenger's window. At this point steer, quickly to the left, turning the steering wheel completely, carry on with the observations as before but this time as you are about to become in line with the kerb take off all your steering lock a fraction early so that by the time you have got all your lock off you should then be straight with the kerb, then as before keep reversing back 3-4 car lengths.

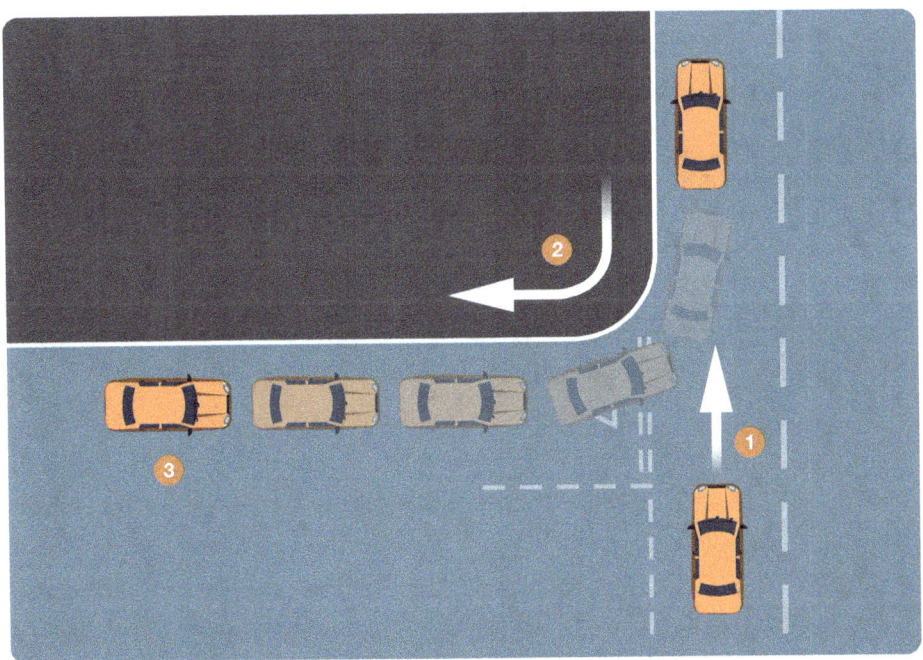

HELP – DON'T HINDER

THE MANOEUVRES

③ REVERSE PARALLEL PARK

This manoeuvre was designed to park your car in between 2 cars or a limited space.

The most common question I'm asked is, "why not drive straight in? The answer is simple, your car that has steering wheels at the front means, that your back wheels will follow the direction of your front wheels, so as you steer the car hard to the left in the forward direction the middle and back of the car will follow to the left and will hit the car beside you.

So, to park you need to drive forward enough not to hit the car beside you which means you have now lost much needed space to park. However, if you pull up past a car so you are slightly over shooting the car but remain parallel to it, we are then in a great position to start this manoeuvre.

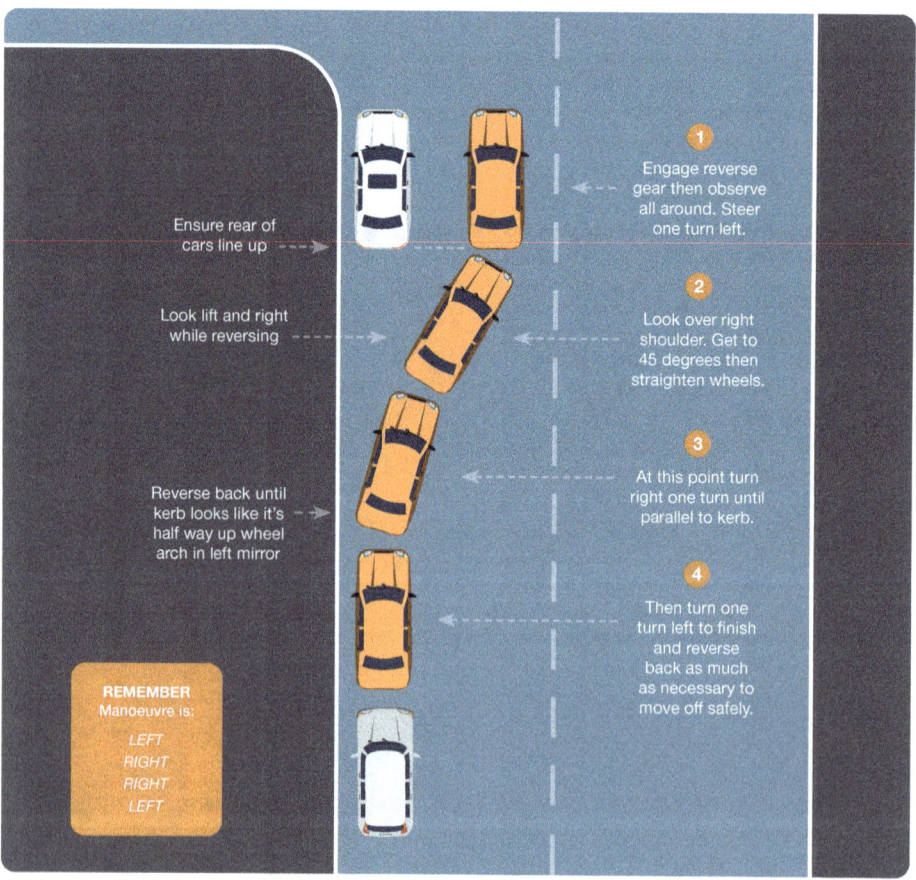

HELP – DON'T HINDER

THE MANOEUVRES

- Select reverse gear as soon as you pause. (This gets the reverse lights on so people from behind are aware of what you are doing). If traffic is coming from either front or rear before you get to pause, apply left indicator.
- Apply hand break to secure car and find biting point.
- All round observation is now required, starting with right shoulder, checking mirrors, road ahead, and over left shoulder (being your last check as it's the direction of travel!)
- If all clear or traffic has stopped, then release handbrake and reverse till the back of your car is in line with the parked car, whilst looking over your left shoulder through rear passenger window. **If you see any traffic coming from any direction then you must stop, remember you are the hazard.**
- My advice would then be to turn the steering wheel quickly 1 full turn to the left, you will notice at this point the front of the car is swinging out to the right, this would be a great opportunity to have an effective look over the right shoulder to see if any further traffic is trying to overtake! As you bring your head back around you want to see the car's angle, of between 35-45 degrees (imagine a clock face, 12 O'clock being your original position now being 1 O'clock but not quite 2 O'clock).
- Take off the turn you put on (now 1 full turn to your right) so your wheels are now straight.
- Looking behind, over your left shoulder and right shoulder, continuously, whilst reversing, until you see in your left exterior mirror, the start of the kerb from the roadside appear, approximately halfway down your rear nearside wheel **(if any traffic starts overtaking you now keep moving back as you are retracting yourself from being a hazard!)** and steer 1 full turn to your right again, this time the front of your car will swing to the left, look at the car in front and when you see you are very nearly straight, steer 1 full turn to your left leaving you 100% straight with the car ahead.
- Continue back a further few feet whilst looking over left shoulder out of rear window in the direction of travel **(once again prepare to pause if traffic is coming, as you are now a moving hazard!)**
- Pause and apply handbrake and neutral to show the Examiner you have finished.
- You should end up about 6-15 inches from the kerb parallel and between 1 and a half to 2 car lengths behind the car in front.

The reason for travelling back a few extra feet is because after the Examiner is amazed at how good your parking was, he would then ask you to move off! You don't want to be in a position where you get too close to the car in front, whilst moving off, especially as it's an angle start where many observations and delicate manoeuvring skills are required.

You are marked on observation and control so take your time, get used to practicing this manoeuvre, and work out when and how long it takes, to look around whilst the car is moving. The biggest fault, from my experience, is people get too much angle and come back and hit the kerb, or they forget about the kerb when coming back and steer to early leaving themselves metres from the curb. Steering the wrong way to start with, you see it doesn't matter if you drive forwards or backwards if your left hand pulls down your car will go left like the start of a circle.

HELP – DON'T HINDER

THE MANOEUVRES

BAY PARKING

Bay parking was brought in by the DVSA as they recognised that there was a need for people to park correctly in shopping centres, etc, due to too many accidents occurring.

So lets start with parking forwards into the bay, which is normally required at the end of each test and in life.

You must have shown good clutch control skills with effective observation, after all lots of people use car parks and are constantly moving around.

Try staying out as wide as possible as this would give you a better turning circle, check your interior mirror followed with either left or right exterior mirror depending which side your parking in, apply a signal to indicate your intention of direction and in a slow controlled movement steer effectively into you desired bay ensuring you are within the bay lines either side coming to a gentle pause.

Apply hand brake and select neutral.

Now if your not satisfied with the straightness or position of your parking, not all is lost, if your engine is off you are permitted to even get out and have a proper look, you can always start the car up again and under control reverse out observing as you go straight back and pull in forwards again and again until you are satisfied. Then and only then will the examiner look at your final result and mark you accordingly.

The main faults to watch out for are: not indicating where appropriate, checking correct mirrors, coming into bay too fast causing sharp breaking, finishing with any wheel still on the bay lines or not being in full control of the car or observations throughout this manoeuvre.

Now reversing into a bay, the same faults as above can occur so be mindful of what you're doing, however the way I teach my pupils this exercise may vary from vehicle to vehicle, but I get pupil to count 3 bays either left or right.

If you were to pick bay 1 then drive past slowly to the furthest line of bay 3 so that it's in line with the middle of your door, pause and apply the handbrake and select reverse gear. Take effective observation around the whole car then steer everything they have to either left of right depending upon the selected bay. Take another look all around, take the handbrake off and reverse slowly backwards maintaining observation all round. This should put the driver on a good course to fitting into the bay. Feel free to use exterior left and right mirrors to help the driver decide when to adjust their steering. Remember they can always pull forward and reverse again if required. Just try to stay wide of the bay on approach as this will have a better turning circle.

Once the driver feels like they have a great idea of what and when steering feels about right try pulling slightly past the drivers reference point of turn and travel backwards and steering on the move, as steering stationary is known as dry steering and whilst is not marked as a steering fault it could cause damage to tyres and steering column over time.

HELP – DON'T HINDER

THE MANOEUVRES

BAY PARKING (FORWARD)

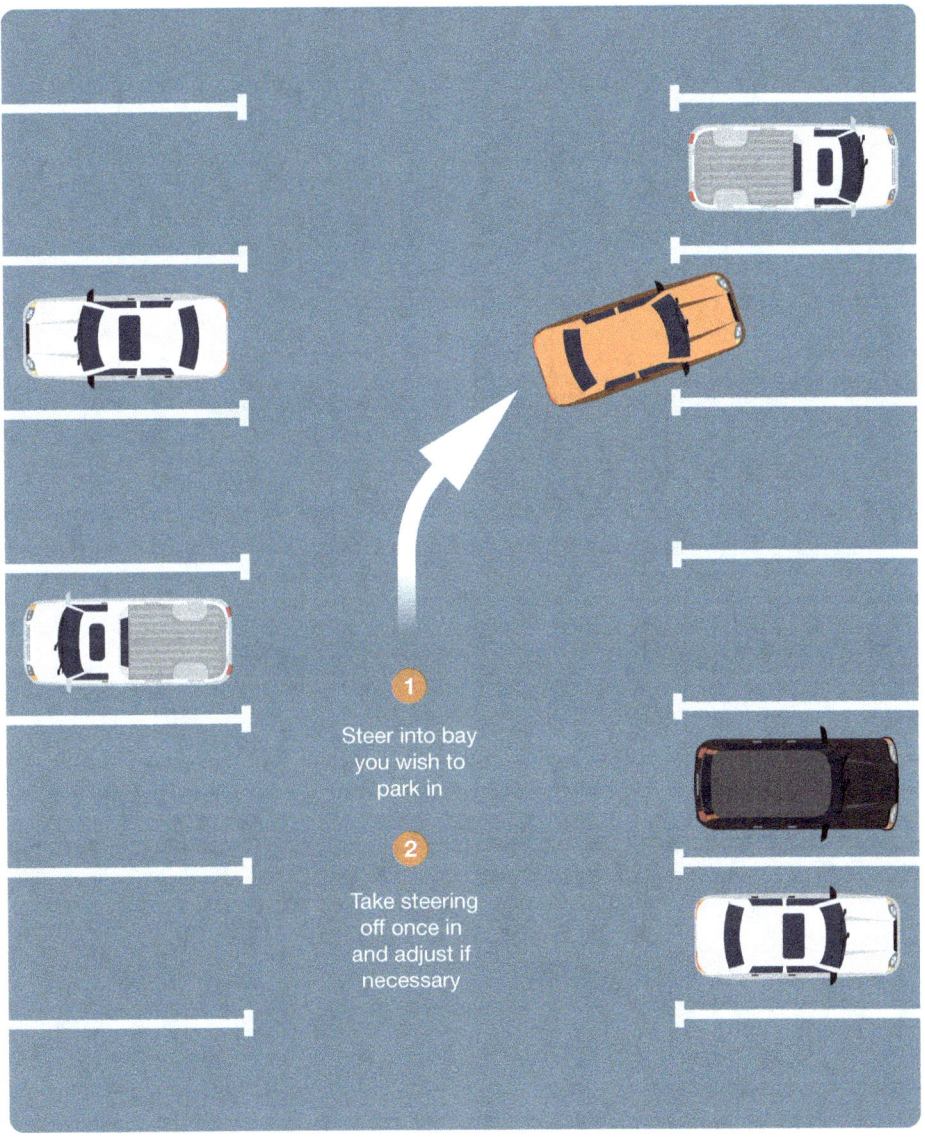

HELP – DON'T HINDER

THE MANOEUVRES

BAY PARKING (REVERSE)

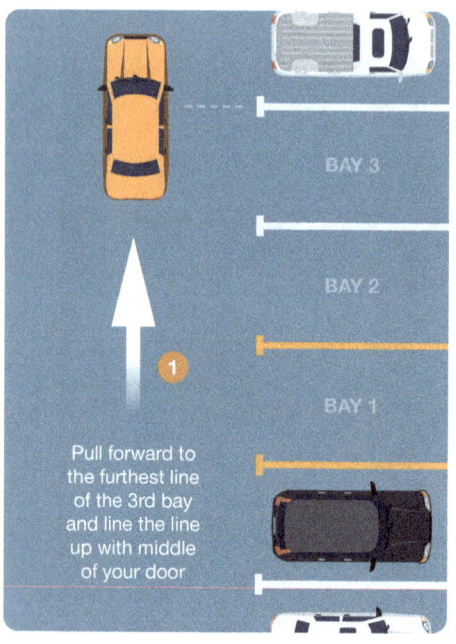

1. Pull forward to the furthest line of the 3rd bay and line the line up with middle of your door

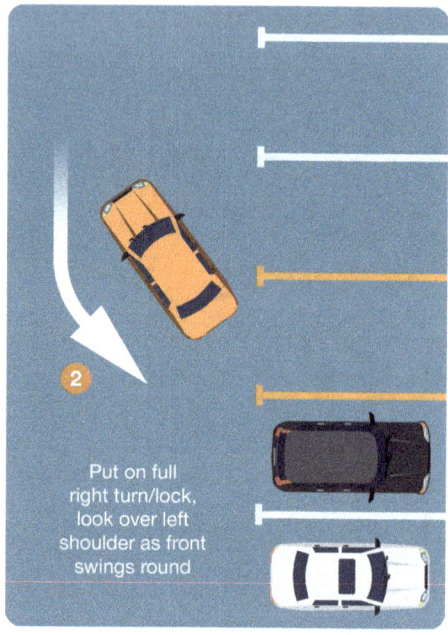

2. Put on full right turn/lock, look over left shoulder as front swings round

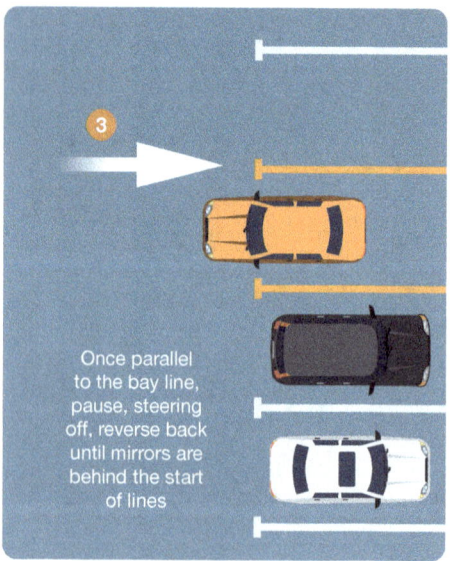

3. Once parallel to the bay line, pause, steering off, reverse back until mirrors are behind the start of lines

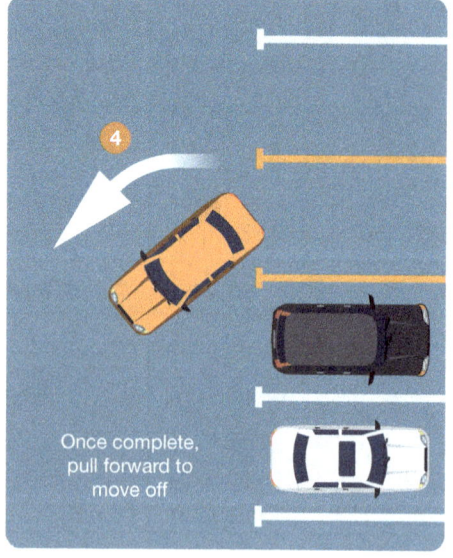

4. Once complete, pull forward to move off

THE MANOEUVRES

5 PARK ON THE RIGHT & REVERSE

This manoeuvre is a new addition to the DVSA test. As more traffic is on our roads and people now park on either side of the road the DVSA wants to ensure learners can pull over to the right, park up safely, reverse back if needed and move off again safely. So what is expected?

You are driving along a road and the examiner will ask you to pull up on the right in a safe convenient and legal place, this doesn't mean right now!! It means when it is safe, with no on coming vehicles that may have to take evasive action or even have to think about what you're up to, legal – so not stopping on road markings/signs prohibiting you to park and convenient so not blocking driveways, bus stops etc.

So have a good look ahead, find a desired place, check main rear view mirror and right exterior mirror, indicate if necessary and come over to the right hand side, slowly reducing speed over 2-5 car lengths until you gently come to rest parallel with the kerb.

You will then be asked to reverse back approximately 2 car lengths, so select reverse gear and give all round observation.

HELP – DON'T HINDER

EMERGENCY STOP

As a good driver, it is very rare that we would ever need to stop in an emergency, because we read the road ahead recognizing potential hazards developing and can anticipate what's going to happen and automatically have a plan of action ourselves if in the event something were to happen. What we do is **look, assess, decide and then act (LADA)**.

Firstly, you see the potential hazard, then in an instant your brain assesses the situation, then you make an educated and calculated decision based on all the knowledge. What's behind you? How close is the vehicle behind you? Can you move over to the left, or right? Do I speed up? Slow down? Maintain speed? etc. And then we act, taking everything above into consideration, the more road experience we have the faster this action is.

Now we can't teach pupils all the situations as these are ongoing, but getting some road miles behind you and putting the pupil into typical situations that we encounter daily would build up their knowledge and confidence, which ultimately speeds up their reaction, and their experience will accelerate quicker when they see different, but similar, situations arise. A good starting point for this may be small roads in a housing estate with parked vehicles either side of the roads with cross roads and T-junctions and side roads all around, so the pupil is having to anticipate what is likely to happen, and of course act when something does happen. If nothing happens then pull over and open conversation, manufacturing situations so they are thinking on the right lines, or better still spot faults other drivers make and ask them what they thought the fault might be? And ask them **why** that may be considered as a fault? And, endeavour to see if they know how to correct that mistake.

However, **do not** throw them in the deep end start off slowly, talk them through lots of roads and talk through situations that are developing, then very slowly reduce the talk through but always be ready! Tell them what they should be looking for, how far ahead, tell them where you are looking and explain there should be situations where you look by scanning short, middle and far distances as well as side to side and when to do this. However even though we anticipate a lot of situations sometimes there are just things you can't anticipate, such as branch falling onto the road or deer jumping out from the side of the road or an exhaust pipe flying off the car in front etc.

So, for this reason the examiner from time to time will ask the pupil to carry out this exercise to see if the pupil can stop the car quickly and under full control. The examiner will ask the pupil to pull over, they would then advise the pupil they are now going to demonstrate their ability to stop the car as if in an emergency, and the signal will consist of the examiner raising their hand and vocally saying **stop**. Now at this stage the pupil knows what's going to happen, and the pupil should also feel a little reassurance of when the examiner will give the command as normally the examiner will check over his shoulder just prior to giving the command to ensure it is safe from following traffic.

Make sure the pupil remembers to move off safely and try to get the car up to the speed of the road, when hearing this command the pupil should come off the gas pedal and apply foot-brake firmly and progressively and at the same time depress the clutch pedal fully (Note: check the car manual for the car your test will be in or any other car you may drive, as some cars require you to put the clutch in at last minute).

Or could be at the same time 'clutch & brake'. Explain to them about **ABS (anti-lock braking system)** Does the car you are driving have this?

THE MANOEUVRES

The way I explain ABS is simply "when we brake hard everything inside the car is travelling at the speed at time of braking, so as the car slows down rapidly everything inside the car is thrown forward, as the front wheels of the car are the last point of contact to the ground we have a tremendous amount of downward pressure on those front wheels that get driven into the ground causing them to lock (not revolve) which in turn means skidding/ sliding.

What the ABS does is recognizes that pressure on the front wheels and as the wheels lock the ABS mechanism automatically releases the brakes to continue to revolve until the wheels lock again and repeats this action until the car has physically stopped, this works very fast indeed and in most cars, makes a grinding noise, (if you do hear this it is okay just keep braking as you are!

If your car does not have ABS then when braking hard you find the car skidding then come off the brake and re-apply progressive braking, so you deliberately allow the wheels to unlock ensuring you re-apply the brakes again but in a progressive manner not stabbing the brake pedal, this action is known as **CADENCE BRAKING.** And if you have skidded then whilst skidding always steer into the skid. (ie: if the back of the car slides to the right then steer to the right, etc.) However, word of warning, do not over steer as this could induce a skid in the opposite direction.

Once your car has stopped in a nice straight line as you had held the steering firm whilst braking apply the hand brake as soon as all four wheels have stopped and select 1st gear then check left then right shoulder before continuing your journey. This is because it is unlikely you have stopped in a normal parking position, normally you're in your normal driving position and traffic from behind could overtake either side etc.

When practising this look at the road condition (loose chippings, mud, water, etc.) as this also needs to be in the front of the mind and be taken into account before a situation happens. Also do not carry out this exercise on bends or around lots of vehicles.

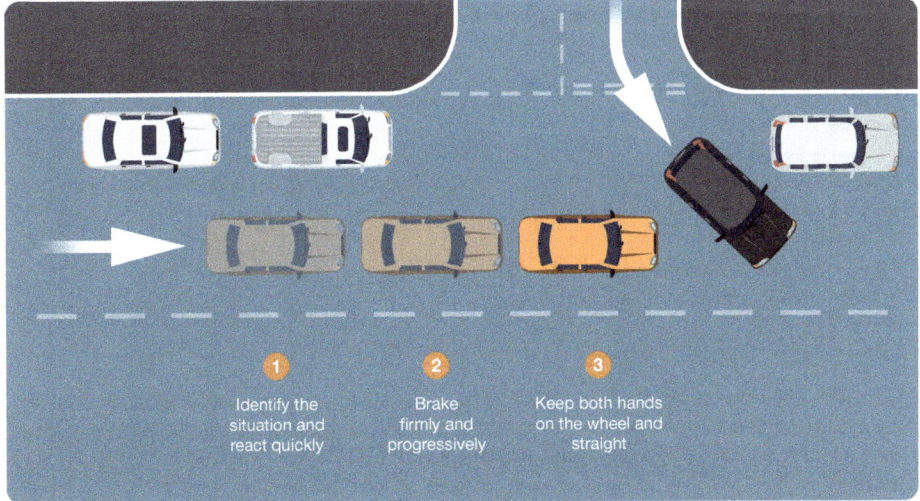

1. Identify the situation and react quickly
2. Brake firmly and progressively
3. Keep both hands on the wheel and straight

HELP – DON'T HINDER

Techniques and Faults

As you can appreciate, when learning to drive, normal road procedures, and situations with roads and traffic, are evolving every second, very rarely is a road the same every time you drive on it, for example your position, or speed may differ, as well as parked or moving traffic being in the same place as previously.

So, I think it is best to teach using **similar situations**. By breaking roads into groups like **town centre, dual carriage ways, country roads, and urban areas** we can then target specific areas for that lesson plan. Below I will aim to select as many faults or tactical procedures in each of the four groups that I have highlighted above.

TOWN CENTRES

This is probably the biggest area for tactics and faults due to the volume of traffic, people, and general obstructions, so what are we dealing with exactly?

Let's break this area down more, so we have:

- Pedestrian crossings
- Roundabouts
- T-junctions
- Cross roads
- Schools and shops
- Buses and taxi lanes and pedestrian priorities
- Traffic calming measures (speed humps etc.)
- One way systems

So let's deal with some of these in turn, what they are and how to deal with them! Pedestrian crossings come in different formats; we have zebra crossings, pelican crossings, toucan crossings, puffin crossings, traffic light controlled cross roads crossings, Pegasus/equestrian crossings. We shall start with the zebra crossing.

THE ZEBRA CROSSING

On approaching any pedestrian crossing my general rule to learners is to look ahead for signs, 'traffic lights' or in the zebras case 'Belisha beacons' or 'lolly pops' that flash on the end of a black and white post either side of the road, upon seeing this I ask pupils to observe in the rear-view mirror the following traffic, so to be able to calculate when to slow down, and how quick, depending on what they see following, then ease off the gas to generate good time to observe either side of the road for anybody wishing to cross, or anticipating somebody's actions on the approach, if all is clear then they have shown good awareness of the crossing and can soon get back to the speed of the road and traffic conditions, however if the crossing has people waiting to cross then the driver needs to pause the car at the single white line before the black and white markings on the road.

Please be advised that older people tend to stand further back and be mindful of people walking towards the crossing, as you don't want to brake suddenly last minute. Never wave people across, you might think you are being kind, but if you do this you could be in a situation where you were deemed responsible for them crossing which can cause problems if something else came and ran them over, somebody would say you told them it was safe 'potentially aiding and abetting in manslaughter I guess?'

When pedestrians do cross let them get all the way to the other side completely before moving off as they could suddenly turn around and walk back.

If it's a double zebra crossing i.e. two lanes going and two lanes coming with an island in the middle, then treat this as two separate crossings.

If a pedestrian at the crossing looks a little sheepish and starts looking in different directions it's fair to say they may have stopped at the crossing not realising traffic had stopped for him, no problem, you have given him the opportunity to cross then carry on driving, just confirming first of course that there is room on the other side of the crossing to go, as you must leave the crossing clear and can see tyres to tarmac of the vehicle ahead always.

On all pedestrian crossings, you also have 'zigzag' lines which lead up to – and slightly past – a pedestrian crossing.

You must not park in these areas as visibility should not be obstructed nor obscured in any way. Extra care is required when changing lanes as well, this should only happen before or after the 'zigzag' crossing.

We should not overtake the lead vehicle on the approach, however if somebody has parked in this area we don't want to hold up traffic unnecessarily. Try and make progress to keep traffic moving, but if the traffic does slow down then change down a gear and make extra observation in front of the vehicle, where people could walk out.

The examiner will recognize the fact that 'actions speak louder than words', so he will see your knowledge of all situations from how you read the road ahead, your observation skills using a scanning technique looking short middle and far distances whilst also checking left and right.

TECHNIQUES AND FAULTS

The ability to anticipate what others are doing and reacting in good time which in turn should give you a continued confidence and pleasure knowing you are driving well, confidence builds confidence and satisfaction.

A USEFUL TIP: give the slowing down arm signal on the approach, this not only advises oncoming traffic that you are preparing to stop for the zebra crossing, but also to advise the pedestrians that you are about to give way.

THE PELICAN CROSSING

As you drive towards this crossing you may well be greeted with the warning triangle sign for pedestrian crossing ahead, as with zebra crossings. On recognising the crossing, you should check your rear view mirror and ease off your gas, this will give you more information about the traffic behind you which in turn could dictate how hard or how soon to brake. It will also make you aware that as this crossing has traffic lights, you can anticipate when the lights are likely to change!

The sequence of this traffic lights is a little different to normal traffic lights, a normal set of traffic lights run from: RED, RED & AMBER, GREEN, AMBER, RED, whereas pelican lights have replaced the RED & AMBER lights with FLASHING AMBER which means if the crossing is clear you may proceed without the lights returning to green.

So as an example you could show how to anticipate the lights by observing the crossing on the approach. As you see people walking towards the crossing check your main mirror, ease off the gas pedal. You will see the pedestrian press the button at the crossing, your car is now engine braking as you enter the zigzag area and the lights change from green to amber but you have already slowed down and can come to a gentle pause as the lights go to red as opposed to "aah flaming heck the lights just changed". This has caught out most drivers from time to time (human error).

Scanning both sides of the crossing for any potential users waiting or approaching and try and anticipate the change of lights which in turn will make your driving smoother, better for passenger's and the car itself and better for traffic flow should be second nature to most experienced drivers and is the very reason I adopt all these key points into a lesson once I have given the briefing. Prevention is better than the cure. When giving briefings, try to geographically place yourself near to where the briefings can be put into practice.

THE TOUCAN, PUFFIN AND EQUESTRIAN CROSSING

These crossings are all organised by a normal sequence of lights. Please ensure you have allowed all persons to reach the other side of the crossing before you commence on your journey.

The toucan crossing is identified by the fact that cyclists don't have to dismount and there are normally cycle lanes on one or more sides of the paths.

Puffin crossings are harder to spot but basically operate via sensors and infrared cameras that start the sequence of lights when pedestrians are in the immediate facility and equestrian or Pegasus crossings are designed for people on horseback so would have a button higher than normal so riders don't have to dismount to operate the crossing, naturally please refrain from revving the engine or sounding your horn when in use!

OTHER TYPES OF CROSSINGS

On some traffic light controlled cross roads you may see your stop line and in front further road markings for pedestrians to cross, you must wait till the pedestrian has fully crossed before you proceed, even if the lights go to green and the driver behind is beeping!

Sometimes you may come across little islands in the middle of the road; this is basically a haven for pedestrians to get too, just to make it easier to cross as perhaps the road is hard for a pedestrian to judge the speed or distance of oncoming vehicles both ways in one go.

We also have to think about traffic calming measures, normally in place where there may be a higher population or residency area or renowned areas of risk to people wanting to cross, these can take many forms like humps in the road, narrowing of the road in various places with priority and give way signs, rumble strips or simply reduce speed signs/ road markings. Either way, whatever form they take it is designed for you to bring your speed down to a reasonable level so you can drive safely with a heightened alertness due to popular hazards, remember driving is a privilege not a priority!

I personally think whether you see the traffic calming measures or not when you come from a lower hazardous environment to a somewhat busier area you need to forward plan, ask yourself what if!

Use scanning techniques looking far, middle and short distances, but also think about prevention before the cure policy i.e. before driving into a situation like overtaking a parked vehicle for example acting as soon as you see the parked vehicle, checking your mirrors, consider a signal as you will overtake at some point then slowing down but maintaining a suitable speed once slowed taking time to see further up the road to assess the future hazards as opposed to slowing down last minute or making the last minute decision your main decision, naturally in this example if you did see the parked vehicle well in advance you may find positioning early to overtake will reduce the use of giving a signal as your position is a signal in its self.

Acting last minute will generate an unnecessary stress of which can affect you in many ways. This is worth talking about in more detail and in far more depth.

DRIVING STRESS EXPLAINED

We all have stress in our lives, but there are many stresses which affect us in many ways, sometimes you can thrive on stress and others can lead you to making lots of small bad decisions ultimately becoming a crisis.

When driving, you are multi-tasking, micro managing many things at once. For example: you are driving along the road to drop children at school, the 2 children are asking you to turn up the radio that you are listening to, and you have speed humps in the road as the speed decreases to 20mph.

TECHNIQUES AND FAULTS

Now let's have a closer look at these key features:

> **School** = lots of cars parking, kids everywhere, lolly pop man, people rushing
>
> **Children talking** = possibly over each other, argument likely
>
> **Radio on and volume switch turning up** = extra noise in background, one hand on steering wheel
>
> **Speed humps** = slowing down, checking mirrors, changing gear perhaps, off the gas on the brake pedals, acting on what's happening and around you from other road users
>
> **New speed** = monitoring new speed looking from the road back to speedometer
>
> And **then it starts to rain**... and so on

So naturally you are more at risk compared with somebody else whom are more focused on their primary job of just driving the car. This stress is taken away when you are focused on the anticipation of hazards. Even though your brain processes all this information and in a way, we program our brain for set drills, for example MSM/PSGL (mirrors signal manoeuvre / position speed gear look) every time we turn into new roads or approach hazards.

On roundabouts we use the hazard drill MSM/PSGL but also use LADA (look, assess, decide, act) so in advance we micro manage a pre-set planned drill. But you imagine how much driving stress is created when for that spilt second our focus has been compromised, our brain becomes overwhelmed, can't compute, we freeze up, or we take an uncharted risk...

Don't ever think that by taking a risk is helping somebody else out, that's known as Noble cause risk taking; think about your consequences on others as well as yourself.

This could then be magnified dramatically if you are late for work and are on a last warning, and if you're sacked you will lose the house because financially you're in trouble and if that happens your wife or husband will leave you and none of the above makes sense because you only had 2 hours sleep because of the new born baby keeping you up all night... life can get to all of us, but learn to find what your own personal stresses are and take practical steps to eliminate them.

Even on a daily basis with my pupils with no real stress make these noble cause risks, a great example is simply there are cars on my side of the road, pupil looks ahead sees a car miles away, decides to make progress and overtake, as he overtakes this longer line of cars than first thought sees the oncoming car closer than anticipated so starts increasing his speed to get passed these cars that in his mind he shouldn't have over taken in the first place, to let this oncoming car to continue without slowing down....

So, let's now break down his thinking, what mistakes did he make I asked?

He answered:

1. Oh I shouldn't have overtaken in the first place he said, not true I said based on what you could see you made the right decision by making progress!

2. Ermm don't know he said...showing me he clearly didn't see the real faults, he thought he was doing the other driver a favour!

TECHNIQUES AND FAULTS

So, I asked him why **he didn't check his rear view and left exterior mirror before he moved back over?** Didn't have time he said! **Going too fast** he said! So now highlighting going too fast past potential hazards, for the road traffic and weather conditions, not anticipating the dangers of doors opening, kids crossing etc. and allowing appropriate time to deal with any given situation, so his **risk assessment was abandoned.**

I asked him what would he do if he saw a car overtaking some cars before we got there and saw there was no room for him to move into? He quite rightly said, "I would **slow down and pause and leave enough room** for the car to get back **safely** to his side of the road"

So, the natural next question that was thrown in was, "what do you think the other driver would have been more than happy to do?" The penny dropped! So, in this noble cause he recognized there should be no noble cause as it shouldn't exist, he should base his thinking on the correct perception of the driving rules, with his own **responsibility and accountability of his very own actions based on the risk assessment he continually makes as the progression of his journey unravels.**

My advice is when getting in the car leave all other baggage out! Don't think about problems beforehand, work, relationships etc. Set the car up properly as per the cockpit drill, be comfortable. Take full responsibility for your own decision-making and forget about previous errors.

Allow enough time for your journey, don't become intolerant or impatient, impulsive or frustrated, these will always exist, it's how you deal with the negative things in your life, not let them take over your life.

One well known type of stress is Red Mist; this is where you have compromised your emotional state of mind and your psychology. You have focused all your attention on getting somewhere quick, chasing the car in front, or any such thing that stops you from being that driver who reads all potential hazards on that journey.

In my life, I have found that anger and frustration is the most common link to this. I have always, and always will teach driving is a privilege…not a priority.

I instil very high standards into each one of my pupils and explain they are like Ambassadors to the road, they are to set an example to each road user out there as they are the most freshly trained and current drivers, however learning never stops, things have and always will change, stay in touch with evolving road craft skills, be kind and considerate to all motorists and maintain what has been taught.

ROUNDABOUTS

What are roundabouts? Why do we have them? One or two questions asked by my pupils regularly, well may I answer by saying at the end of the road you may be faced with an island of a circular orientation in most cases that have roads coming off for different directions, they are designed to allow traffic to flow where possible to ease congestion.

The drivers coming from the right have priority over us, but we may proceed if our actions don't cause other vehicles to slow down or take evasive action.

Please refer to the following diagram:

HELP – DON'T HINDER

TECHNIQUES AND FAULTS

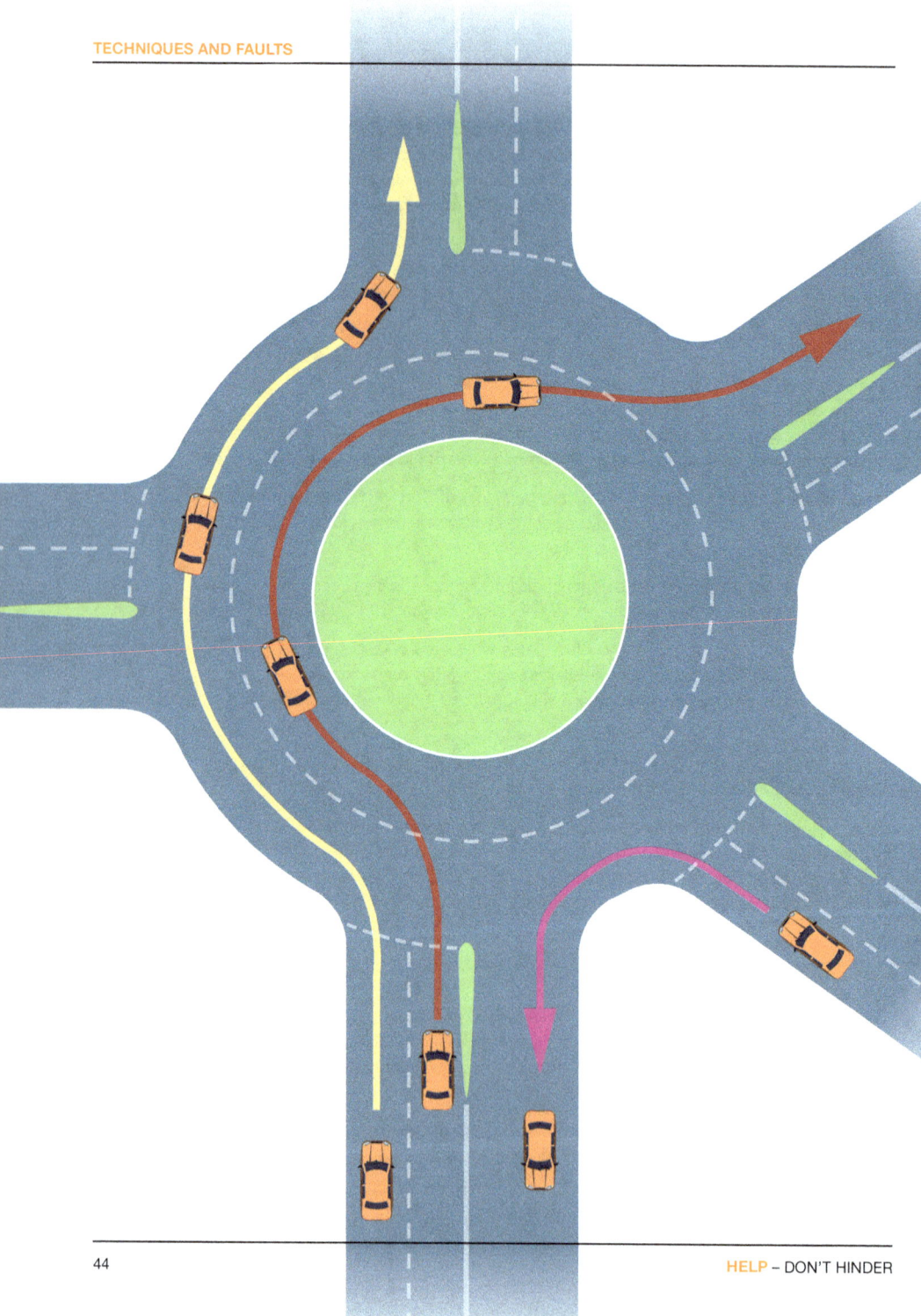

HELP – DON'T HINDER

Now the way I teach this is by explaining to the pupil that if our preparation is good it will make the ability to judge and decide a whole lot easier.

So, to start with we use our hazard drill upon seeing the round-a-bout sign coming up, or satellite navigation or verbal commands by instructor or examiner, on gaining the information for your destination we will start using the **MSM / PSGL routine**. (Hazard drill)

Look at the map of the roundabout, we are approaching from the bottom towards the junction, see how many exits the junction has coming off, let's use our diagram for this, we have 4 exits, 1st exit is going left, as we always go clockwise, so treat the map as a clock!

2nd exit looks straight ahead or 12 o'clock, 3rd exit is right or 2 o'clock and the 4th exit almost goes back the way we have just come.

So, let's deal with taking the 1st exit left.

Using our hazard drill, the first thing is M.

M for mirrors, checking your interior mirror followed by a directional mirror, we need to assess the following traffic to see how close they are to us, which in turn allows us to make the decision when and how to slow our vehicle down shortly followed by the left exterior mirror to assess what's beside us, ensuring it is safe for use to continue as planned.

Next is S. S is for signal, to alert other road users of our intentions, so they can plan what they want to do or act on what we are planning to achieve.

M. M is for manoeuvre which I have broken down into four other letters **PSGL** which means **P** is for position, if we are going anywhere before 12 o'clock (straight ahead) then unless road signs or road markings state otherwise we normally position the car to the left, our normal road position (2 feet from the kerb or edge of carriageway markings) but at this stage we are still approaching the roundabout quickly

It is around this time I ask pupils to now have a look to the right, this is the traffic we will need to give way to, but all I want from them is an assessment of where the main flow of traffic is coming from and going to. For example, is the traffic coming from our 3rd exit going to our 1st exit, or, from our 2nd exit to our 4th exit or further round, or is there vehicles coming from all directions,

That initial assessment, generates an understanding of the developing situation you are coming into, and the likelihood that we could go or stop, with this assessment we could say instead of looking at traffic we could look for gaps-opportunities this way we would be more focused on trying to make progress as opposed to: oh there's a car I had better stop!

This is where the **S** comes in for speed, we must give way to the right, so let's slow the car down to a suitable speed not just to get onto the roundabout but for the duration of our left turn to avoid over or under steering and to maintain a great road position and secondly to allow us time for another assessment of the developing traffic, I would normally ask the pupils to slow down to about 10 / 15 mph, as they slow down it is here when **G** for gear comes in.

Depending on the vehicle you're driving you may need to read about gears and speeds but in most cars I find 2nd gear is normally best, and once again this gear change ideally wants to be done with the clutch up so the driver has a good amount of time to make the decision to either go or stop, there is nothing wrong at this point if the round-about has a gap for the driver to either speed up a little or decelerate to fit into the gap, but my last letter is **L** which is for the final look, this is to confirm that his last assessment was correct, to be in time to stop before the roundabout smoothly.

Now if we want to go straight ahead at the round-about, just check your main mirror, no signal required as you're not going left or right, stay in your normal road position (unless road markings/signs say otherwise) follow the rest of your hazard drill as everything is the same, but instead of steering down the road to your left, steer the car round staying close to the left in your lane checking your interior mirror followed by your left exterior left mirror and apply your left signal when its either obvious you're not turning left 1st exit or when you are level with the middle of your 1st exit, this way you maximise your intentions to all other road users, (if you delayed your signal past the last exit then examiners would be correct in marking you down on your test for a timing fault).

Then simply follow your lane off the roundabout looking for new speed signs and checking your interior mirror as you are now in a new road.

This time we are turning right at the roundabout, anything past 12 o'clock is classed as a right turn! So once again, on seeing the map of the roundabout, check your interior mirror followed by your right exterior mirror applying your right signal, check your right mirror again to confirm no one has started overtaking you then position yourself just left of the centre of the road or in your right lane. The 'speed, gear, look' part of your hazard drill is exactly the same, but when you choose to enter the roundabout position the car close to the roundabout following it clockwise, stay in this position until you are nearly level with the exit you don't wish, check your interior mirror, left mirror, and if time allows look over your left shoulder to confirm room to come over, signal left and start coming away from the roundabout making a bee line for your new road position, if you are direct with your actions then this will be seen as a signal, confirmation of what you are doing, as your position is a signal, other road users will find this helpful in their decision-making as you would if someone was doing this for you.

Now there are tell tail signs (clues) to what the traffic is likely to be doing, but these clues are not made in stone as drivers change their minds.

After assessing where the main flow of traffic is coming from, have a look at your 3rd exit. Ask yourself: are there any cars approaching? If yes, then are they slowing down creating a potential gap? If the answer is yes again, asking yourself why? Is it because they are giving way to their right?

If so, are the cars they are giving way to, staying close to the roundabout, or travelling on the outside? If they are close to the roundabout they are likely to continue to come around, if not, then they are more likely to be coming off before they get to you. Are they signalling? Where are they looking? Does the car that's close to the roundabout look like he is getting wider from it near your 3rd exit, he could be coming off! The same as you if you were taking your 3rd exit!

But in short look and identify signals, progressive position and where are they looking.

The opposite diagram shows a combination of lanes and positions that could occur, run through in your mind clearly what procedure would you use for each situation.

TECHNIQUES AND FAULTS

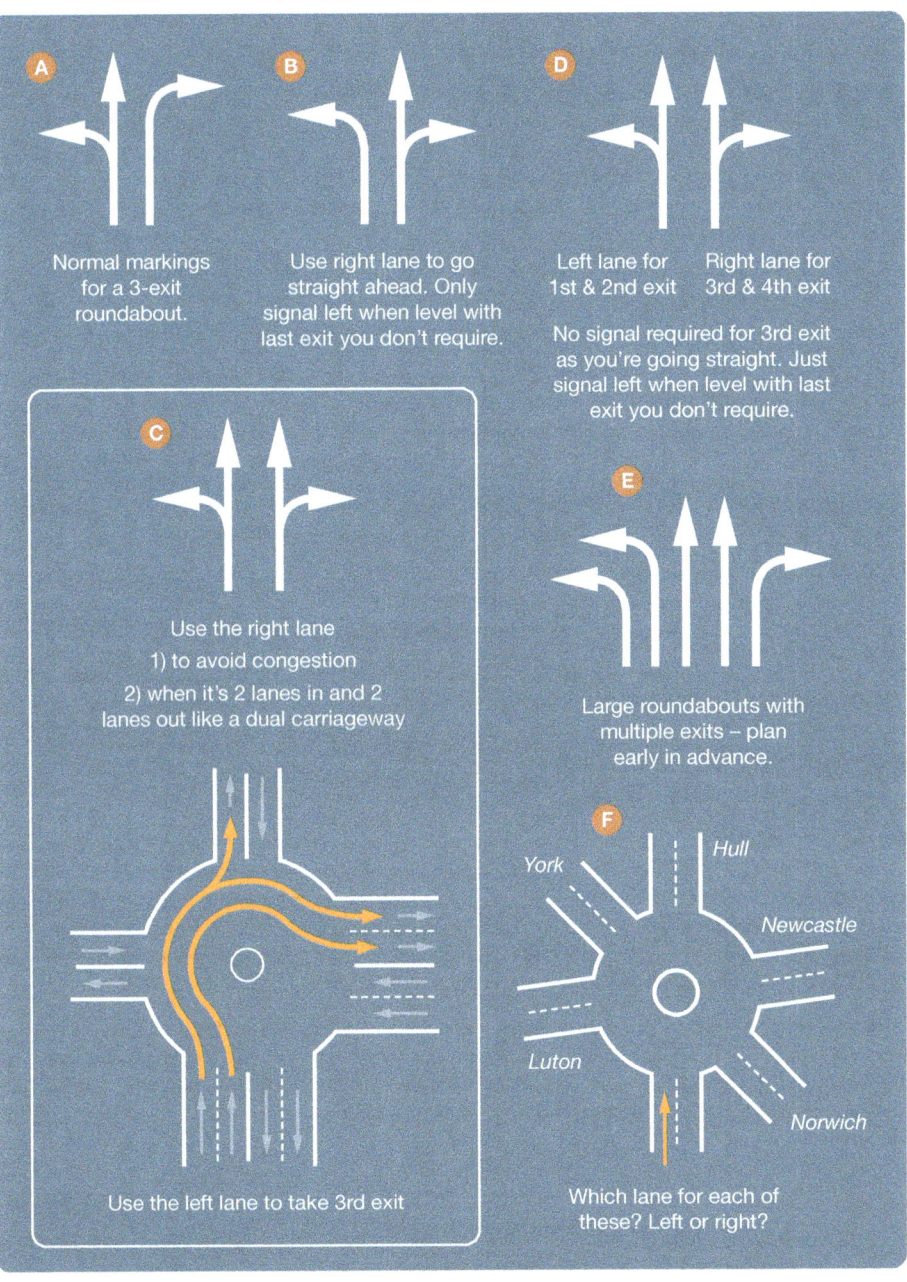

HELP – DON'T HINDER

TECHNIQUES AND FAULTS

There are other types of roundabout, mini and spiral.

Mini round abouts vary in size, sometimes they are only marked with road paint, sometimes slightly raised with road markings the same as another give way or stop hazard lines, the procedure is the same for turning left, however if you are going straight across or to the right you don't have to worry about applying your left signal, the reason for this is that the time you check your mirrors and apply the signal you would most likely to be in the road that you wanted, I haven't ever had pupils get marked down for signalling or not by examiners when exiting mini round about.

Spiral round about are the same as normal roundabout but with extra road markings to aid drivers going around to the right to be able to move across a lane to the left every time there is an exit to the left, so basically as a vehicle leaves, vehicles from other lanes come across one, so eventually you would have moved across to the left by the time you have reached your desired exit,

TIP: if the examiner asks you to follow the signs for... college for example, this would be local traffic normally highlighted on white board with black writing displayed on the main traffic sign or before the main sign.

Which means if he said London for example look for main board you don't always have time to read every direction. The earlier you react the better and more confident the roundabout will become.

If you do stop at around about, plan your 1st to 2nd gear change, without disruption to your signalling, on large round about pull away and make progress with a nice early gear change, small roundabout don't put yourself in a position where you are changing gear when that signal should be going on.

Also, keep an ear out for emergency vehicles, allow them full access to the round about as much as you can! If you are on the roundabout and an emergency vehicle is coming from your left, slow down and stop, let them be in front of you.

If that's too late, then make room for them as quickly and as safely as you can, remember they want to get to their emergency quickly, not attend you because you panicked and crashed.

Make sure you stay in the correct lane, no straddling from one lane to another, as this could be marked as a lane discipline fault, or a steering fault, road position fault, or even an awareness and planning fault. If you've shown a high definition of the lane, that in itself is a signal to other road users and if you find you're in the wrong lane for your desired destination then, unless you can move across carrying out the necessary safety observations, I would continue the wrong way. You can always turn around somewhere else and cause other drivers less stress than doing something wrong on the roundabout.

However it is worth mentioning that on your approach to the roundabout you don't show hesitation, you shouldn't slow down unnecessarily, act on what you see, remember cars behind you will also be assessing the situation and will potentially want to accelerate to maintain their progress. Don't hold them up otherwise the examiner will be inclined to assess this as a hesitation fault.

T-JUNCTIONS

T-Junctions are called T-Junctions because they are shaped like the letter T. The way I teach these junctions is by first separating them into 2 types of junction, OPEN and CLOSED.

I am referring to the zone of vision on the approach; an open junction is where you can see clearly in both directions on the approach.

Closed junctions either have impaired vision from either side looking left or right, or altogether. Depending on what you can effectively see on the approach will dictate the speed and in turn gears to be used.

You should always use you hazard drill on the approach (MSM / PSGL) but by assessing what sort of junction it is, will allow you to potentially calculate the likelihood of being able to continue or not at the end of the road, so for example, you could see in advance that the junction is a closed junction, because of houses, bushes, trees, cars, stop signs, etc... so, you can believe that at an early stage you would be stopping at the end of the road, so by braking progressively and selecting first gear on the approach will put you into a great position to be ready to move off as soon as you have effectively taken good observation both ways, (tip: try practicing looking in the way clearest first, this will give you optimum opportunity to go!).

Naturally if in the event it's a stop sign at the end of the road, then approach in which ever gear you are in as when you stop you will be required to apply the hand brake, secure the car, select first gear and then take effective observations, whether it's a stop sign or not you should always approach smoothly towards the end of the road and gentle pause so the front of the car does not exceed the end of the road.

Nor do you want to stop too far away from the end of the road; a good driver will take care in getting into the correct position.

Every action has a reaction, so you can picture in your mind the effect you would have on cars having priority travelling left or right in front if it were to look like you were approaching too fast and overshooting the end of the junction. Other motorists may take some form of evasive action. Also, during bad weather, the road surface may be wet, with loose stones or even soiled by oil. You may find you cannot physically stop.

Once stopped at a junction you may find you still can't see! If this is the case, then peep and creep, squeeze and ease, terms used by instructors to gently use the clutch on biting point, with very small movements on and off the biting point to control the car to move the car very slowly forwards looking left and right continuously allowing you to pause immediately on seeing another vehicle. If your actions would cause them to slow down or take evasive action, from the examiners point of view, you stopped at the end of the road correctly, took effective observation and started to make progress.

If you have moved slowly into a position that you are satisfied you can continue getting up to the speed of the road without causing other vehicles to slow down or take effective observation, then it appears you have successfully exited from a T-Junction left or right.

The beauty of assessing the type of zone of vision and acting early on this means you will be able to assess what the corner is like when turning left.

If it's a sweeping corner then because you have slowed down and changed down means you should be able to negotiate the corner correctly staying close to the kerb in your normal driving position (2 feet) so you will at least be facing towards the direction of travel, as this will eliminate any chance of turning out wide potentially towards oncoming vehicles.

I find that if it's a sharp corner then knowing how the back wheels may clip the kerb I suggest the pupils try to get their left wing/exterior mirror in line with the left kerb then apply full steering whilst moving

TECHNIQUES AND FAULTS

forward slowly to avoid dry steering. (Dry steering is a term used for steering the car whilst stationary, this causes damage to tyres and steering column).

But also, reminding them to take steering off just before they are straight, so the time it takes to get the steering off they will be straight, otherwise they may find as they are straight then take the steering off they would no longer be straight and on a collision course for the pavement or oncoming traffic depending which way they must steer quickly.

TIP: if going up a hill slip into 1st gear before you get to the end of the road so you can find the biting point whilst you still have momentum thus giving you the opportunity to continue moving if the situation allows.

CROSS ROADS

A cross road is a term used when one road crosses another road like a cross +, there are several types of cross roads of which we will discuss the main ones.

As you drive along a main road you may see a road sign saying there's a crossroads ahead, you may well find you also have road line markings telling you there is a hazard ahead, as you have priority the roads to the left or right they call this a **PRIORITY CROSSROAD**, they may have give way lines / signs of which the other vehicles should abide by, but as a good driver you are aiming to become the best driver you can, to take an accident avoidance technique I suggest to all my pupils to check there rear view mirror to assess the following traffic, ease off the gas pedal and have a look left and right into the roads on the approach to generate an action plan if any other vehicles were potentially going to overshoot their junctions, any information of what's coming out of those roads is knowledge which we can process quickly and take any necessary course of action we see fit.

For example, if I saw a fire engine turning out of junction behind me I could quickly look for somewhere to pull over safely (forward planning and awareness).

If you don't see any road signs continually look for tell tail signs that there might be a cross roads coming up, roads can be hidden by vehicles parked or other obstructions but what you will have is gaps in between parked cars, gaps in between houses or even using your SATNAV if available but in these areas, I use a scanning technique looking ahead long middle and short distances, paying attention to congested or built up areas! If there is a traffic queue ahead make sure you leave the cross roads clear, this will allow room for any emergency vehicles access in and out of the road.

If you are turning left into the road just have a glance to your right before you turn so you have the knowledge that other road users that are coming out of the road to the right won't cause you any disruption to what you are doing, and if they are, at least you will have time to compensate for their errors and avoid any accidents! (Prevention is better than the cure!) And you will be aware of any emergency vehicles that may be joining the same route as you. The same if you are turning right take the time on the approach to look to your left without jeopardising your point of turn that's normal for a right turn.

Now sometimes things can get a little confusing, you wish to turn right and the oncoming car wants to turn right, we think who gets to go first? Well there are two ways to deal with this, **near side to near side or off side to off side.**

TECHNIQUES AND FAULTS

HELP – DON'T HINDER

TECHNIQUES AND FAULTS

Imagine the car parked close to the kerb, the side of the car closest to the kerb is the nearest (known as near side) and the driver's side is the furthest from the kerb so from now on its known as the off side.

The safest way usually is off side to off side, so you move into a position like your point of turn and the driver will pull up beside you to his point of turn, so what you now have is driver beside driver or off side to off side like the diagram shows, you can see the road you are turning into and any further traffic coming towards you clearly and so can he! Allowing you to make your turn safely at the same time if situation allows.

If you use near side to near side, turning in front of each other, be careful, as you can't always see past them and you are considering your road and not the left hand side of your front bumper – neither is he! So, there is a risk on smaller roads you may bump. But the biggest problem is if they wish to move into an off-side position and you don't, it could look like you have just pulled in front of another vehicle! So, make good eye contact with the other driver and try and encourage them to use off side to off side where possible.

Certain situations do call for near side to near side procedure like a staggered cross road where one road is slightly off set to the other, there may be arrows in road telling traffic where to wait.

Look at the diagrams below to help picture the procedure for both!

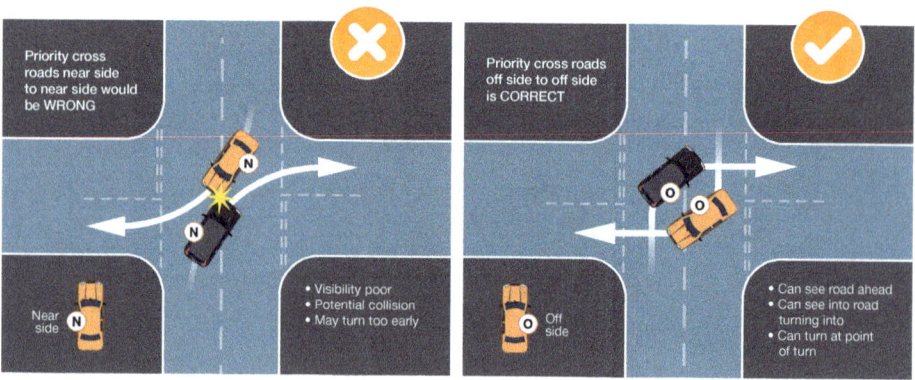

The next cross road is known as a **marked** cross road, as unlike the priority cross road we no longer have priority; we have road markings, either give way or stop.

It's just like approaching the T-Junction except we have an extra road straight ahead or staggered.

So, when turning left, not only do you need your normal observations but you now need to include observation ahead as well. You can go if you don't cause the cars from your right to slow down or take evasive action as you have priority over the car from straight ahead as your movement is easier than theirs, you are simply joining traffic, they should cross lanes and join your traffic, just be aware that vehicles from your left are not already over taking traffic otherwise you could be heading towards a collision if you proceed!

However, a word of warning, if the car straight ahead was there first they may be impatient and try and go! Try and make eye contact once again, be clear in your mind on what the other driver is going to do. Remember it's better to be safe than sorry, yes they may be wrong in their actions but remember driving is a privilege not a priority, prevention is better than the cure.

HELP – DON'T HINDER

When turning right yourself please allow a larger gap in between traffic as you need to not only cross two lanes but also get up to the speed of the road, this all takes time!

Now when going straight at a marked cross road the examiners would expect some forward planning! Before you get to the end of the road look ahead into your new road, ask yourself is there any hazards on your side of the road near the mouth of the junction? If there is then position your car just to the left of the centre of your road, if road is wide enough for two cars side by side, as I would ask you to take the most direct route to get past the hazard, the reason for this is quite

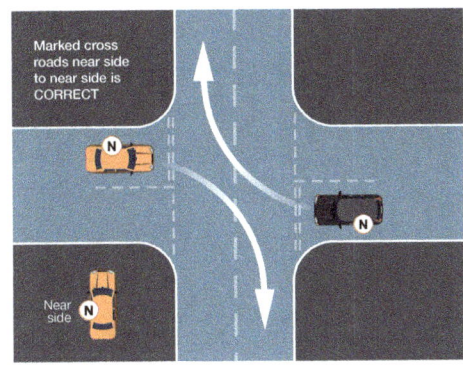

simple, if you drive across the road and pause behind the hazard your vision once again is going to be distorted or limited thus putting you in a more hazardous situation never mind about any new traffic turning in the same road.

Some crossroads have no road markings; this is known as an **unmarked crossroads.**

We would deal with these cautiously! It's not like a roundabout where we give way to the right but more like whoever gets there first would have priority, but be alert as not all drivers may see this to be the case, once again make eye contact and be sure in your mind what other drivers are likely to do!

Just as an example you both get there roughly at the same time and the other driver is looking left and right vigorously and creeping forward, let them go! It doesn't matter, there again they may give a wave of a hand or an acknowledgement head nod, because you are focusing in on them the slightest body language would be understood in a positive form, but still go on your decision from your own judgement, not because someone waves you across.

The last type of crossroads I will bring to your attention is the **traffic light controlled crossroad**, this is a crossed road giving priority to the flow of traffic via the use of traffic lights.

The lights work in a way where you and the traffic opposite you will get the green light to go, but remember, you can't turn in front of oncoming traffic as they have priority because their direction is the easiest manoeuvre so you should position yourself just before your point of turn with your wheels straight, so in the event a vehicle hits you from behind you would simple go straight not being forced into oncoming traffic, and just before your point of turn as if you remember we can't dry steer so this would allow you to steer whilst moving forwards to your actual point of turn.

On some of these intersections there may well be other lanes coming on with filter arrows, just wait at the stop line or if in traffic behind other cars with the 2T's (terminology for tyres to tarmac) this means in stationary traffic position yourself so you can see the vehicles rear tyres to tarmac, because if the vehicles breakdown you can still have enough room to drive around etc....

Be aware of any pedestrian crossings in these areas; if a pedestrian is crossing make sure they have reached the other side before you proceed! Even if your traffic light is on green.

Giving up your right to drive

After teaching lots of people over 60 something has became very clear. Yes, the pupil had become one with the car, but not with the traffic conditions, for what they lacked with good modern road sense they excelled with experience.

What I mean is, they may not be reading the road ahead far enough which means they could apply an **accident avoidance technique** but instead once the hazard became a developing hazard, their experience then took over, allowing them to get out of tricky situations but they missed the point that if they drove differently, there would not have been a tricky situation in the first place! It's very well them sticking their head out of the window and saying to the very fortunate person "you're bloody lucky I missed you sonny Jim" or "it's a good job I braked when I did, one second longer and you would have met your maker" and feeling pleased with themselves that they still have the reflexes to be able to act. Really?

Or is it more like they didn't see the potential hazard till last minute then acted through experience leaving little time for following traffic to react as well potentially causing a pile up and the poor driver that's 5 cars back who hits the car in front gets the blame for driving too close to the car in front? Sure this is a contributing factor but this whole scenario could have been avoided in the 1st place if the older driver continually anticipated the road a head asking "what if?" when assessing the forever evolving road and traffic conditions.

I also found that older drivers were some-what too relaxed… or lazier when it came to lane discipline.

Over 30 years of driving and not having one smack in their car means they have earned the right to drive in any lane on the roundabout if they get to their destination, they have no need to signal as they know where they are going and because they are the front car on approach then it's not affecting any other road user… (in their mind!)

The fact that they are holding up traffic because people can't get passed or people don't emerge onto the roundabout opposite as they don't know if the car is coming around or not just causes confusion as it's not just an indicator that gives an important signal it's the cars position that is a signal too! Causing confusion when the car's position is one that suggests he is coming off and an indicator that says he is staying on, or vice-versa… Hmmmm.

And the trouble is, they get let off the hook each time as if some-one beeps "well it can't be for me!" Or "what an impatient prat, tut" when its everybody else's good driving that's the only reason he hasn't lost his wing mirror or bumper!

Can you hand on heart say you carry the knowledge of all the aspects of driving tactics but also practice these tactics every day in the car, if the answer is an honest NO then at least you recognize some remedial training is needed, if you are unsure ask friends or family members for their opinions or a professional to sit in for a few hours.

GIVING UP YOUR RIGHT TO DRIVE

DO NOT be ignorant and think I'm alright, I only go out once a week, as you may find after being a great mum or dad or well respected pillar of the community, or head of your department or any great stature for many years that in less than 1 minute your whole life and reputation could be turned upside down. Never mind the guilt factor of destroying someone else's life and that of their families for the sake of not listening to friends or family members or even CAR HORNS on a regular basis.

I have spoken to general practitioners (GPs) with regards to the "fitness to drive" question.

This issue has been brought up several times, by some of my pupil's parents that asked me for advice about their parents, and their ongoing concerns.

"How should I approach this concern with my mother or father?"

"Who is the best person for me to speak with?"

"Do you know what other people do when this situation arrives?"

These are just some of the questions that are frequently asked. The only answer I can give is that they know their family member, how do they think they would react?"

Do you have any brothers or sisters and what are their feelings?

What evidence would you use to support this concern?

Can you as two families face this together?

When I asked local GPs, their answer was quite... medically orientated... surprise! If somebody comes to them and they are diagnosed with a condition that affects their driving then okay, the doctors can recommend they don't drive until their medication or fitness to drive has improved. But in most cases where a family member comes to them and say "my dad's driving is bad, I can't get the keys off him I need you to try, then the doctor's response is one of "well I can't, I haven't sat in their car with them, you know their ability far better than me" which is a fair point!

They are not in the business of assessing driving abilities all they can do is a medical and advise patients in confidence how their illness could affect their future to drive.

The onuses are down to the patient to ensure they inform the appropriate authorities of any change to health where they have been deemed unfit to drive, unless the illness is of sort where a medical body must report such findings to the authorities for the patient's safety and safety to others.

The medical association do use books of reference for hundreds of situation illnesses that affect or could affect somebody to drive. So, if you have any real concerns of a family members driving then perhaps contacting DVLA with your concerns in writing may well be the way forward in difficult circumstances.

Most of the time the person would have bumped the car or had little shock which has given families a chance to discuss the future of their driving. Some of the time a situation has been investigated by local police and the driver has been asked to complete a course which makes them think! But most of the time the feedback I have had has been successful as the families have raised the concern with the individual as a family and with rational thinking, backed by a little evidence and love delicately infused, has gained respect and thoughts and keys by the elder.

GIVING UP YOUR RIGHT TO DRIVE

An interesting situation arose earlier this year, a client who had mobility car had the car retrieved 3 days after getting it, he had an accident in previous car 3 times in a short space of time, nothing major until he misunderstood the traffic lights at crossing a dual carriage way, had a major side impact which spun the car around 180 degrees and then a second high impact in the passenger side of which the passenger was hospitalised. Because of the circumstances the insurance company cancelled his policy and recalled the mobility car. After he appealed against their decision, the insurance agreed to this person being able to regain insurance if he was to seek a driving instructor to carry out an assessment, that person was me!

We meet and even though the gentlemen were in his 69th year he omitted to me that he had never had a professional lesson in his life but had passed the driving test some 45 years prior it was clear that having a driving test today he wouldn't have got much further than the test centre!

But what the insurance company asked was for a grading of his ability on some of the aspects required for test, so he turns up in an automatic car when he normally drives manual, with parking sensors and all mod cons, using cruise control constantly to avoid speeding, sat nav for idea of the speed of the road as he didn't have a clue and so on…. Just very desperate to continue to drive, I marked him on their sheet fairly, I then gave extra tuition on the things like why we have mirrors, why we should give 1.5 metres (4 foot) when passing parked vehicles, why we should pause at the end of the road not stopping 1.5 metres (3 foot) over etc. of which in all fairness he took all on board, but the clear message I put to him in all his excitement was, yes at the end of the day in the short space of time that I saw you, you were just about there, but I really recommend you think about having some private tuition, and extra mirrors to compensate your lack of mobility when reversing, but more important to any of this do you really hand on heart think you should be driving, how would you feel now at this time in your life if you hurt someone or took their life, your reputation that you earned all those years in business gone overnight, injuring loved ones worse than you already have, don't wait for this situation to arise, it's not worth it, but you and only you can make that decision, today you still have a licence. I will leave you with that thought.

If it was me I would have gone home and had a long think, to be honest, I can see he wasn't going to listen to me, to him he had passed his test before I was born! I wish him a safe life!!!!

In June 2014 after coaching driving in Lowestoft for nearly 10 years full time I was curious on how my training compared to the rest of the country, after all the only real feedback you receive from the DVSA is when you have your check tests which is once every so often depending upon your grade which varies from weeks up to 4/5 years and even then can be manipulated, for example an Instructor is normally given notice before he has a check test, so he has time to prepare the right pupil, with their best lesson plan, including the route, can practise weeks in advance to then get the best grade they possibly can, to then get left alone to do what he wants for the next 5 years, companies even have massive workshops for people to attend teaching you how to get best grades possible!

Okay so some genuine instructors that want to improve or continue their own development will benefit dramatically from this, unfortunately there are many instructors that may well do great on check test but don't have the right attitude or ability to coach well on a day to day basis giving continuity of quality or professionalism and care to the ever-evolving job.

I personally know far more really great instructors graded 4 or 5 than any 6's. I think the public also saw this over time and then chose RECOMMENDED instructors which is by far the best way, those that are bad

instructors will lose work until they raise their standard, which is always the best learning curve anyone in business can have, its harsh but effective.

As an instructor, I have saved thousands of pounds over the years on advertising, because people talk, word spreads, and when I stop getting referrals I know something is wrong, time to personally reflect, speak to pupils, luckily for me its normally another local instructor has set up and doing an impressive advertising campaign, with hot deals which as a learner you should consider.

The new instructor is fresh, modern trained, enthusiastic, motivated everything is normally good! Time will tell if they stay the course, the only thing they won't have is experience, this can save time, money and your own confidence. But as I have mentioned before the older instructor who has been successful for lots of years may not be in complete touch with new and improved methods of coaching and are normally set in their ways, (not always a bad thing).

So, the time had come for me to see how I was with the much faster pace, the very developed major cities, smart road systems and a massive area including 7 test centres as opposed to my normal 1. West Yorkshire was the place that I had chosen, the areas I covered were: Leeds city and outskirts, Pontefract, Dewsbury, Huddersfield, Bradford, Halifax, Tadcaster, Wakefield and Holmfirth, and everywhere in-between.

Now for most instructors that move to a new area for work they normally focus on getting to know the town's roads, the test centre that's local, find out the routes and practise knowing them, then advertising within a 3-mile radius and hopefully start picking up work bit by bit building up a brand-new reputation bearing in mind the have had no presence in this area before, no networking, no friends or anything.

I can honestly say this is a scary thought, even more so when you have a wife and children in tow! Paying rent from day 1... finding and enrolling children into new schools and ensuring their welfare is tip top.

Once in a while it's good to be taken out of your comfort zone and stretched, and I was no exception, but you do have to limit the awkward situations to stop a crisis from happening. So, firstly my wife gained employment from a private midwifery company, we obtained a good home in a good area for schools, and had them enrolled within a week of being there. Knowing I was starting from scratch, I stood on the shoulders of giants in the industry who had a fantastic reputation built up over for 20+ which was Learner Driver Centre (LDC) of who were my original mentors. After joining the franchise in less than a week my car had new decals, website was built and had 3 intensive courses, 2 semi-intensive courses and around 8 pupils having weekly lessons! So fully booked, within 2 weeks, but to get this I needed to be flexible with areas so by advertising on the web and face book (all free) I covered a much wider area with many thousands more pupils potentially.

By doing a good job, being honest, reliable, clean with a smart appearance, confident proved better than some of those that had been teaching for years, pupils couldn't believe how quickly they progressed, 1st time passes one after the other, pupils ditching their old instructors just to try me out based on what their friends had said. I visited and introduced myself to the test centres, I didn't worry about the test routes as my philosophy was quite simple, train and coach the pupil to drive the car following correct procedures giving them experiences on a massive array of road systems and layouts within an everyday driving environment using client-centred learning, coaching them to recognise and make sound decisions on what they saw.

At the end of twelve months after seeing all but 2 pupils pass one because he didn't get his test booked before I left and the other who did fail but we ran out of time to try again, it was a very successful mission.

I found from self-reflection my SATNAV showed many roads that didn't exist? I was mortified saying to pupils please take your next left, and them saying "really!" You can't get a sheep up there! And they were right, what appears to be a main road was either footpath or impassable dead end.

So naturally you adapt and over come! But I did have some very embarrassing situations, stretching my patience.

However, I do believe that whether you have a professional instructor or family member helping you, you must focus on the substance of the lesson, not the routes or poor quality roads you are on. Works but more importantly what doesn't work? And why? Ask how can I improve? What was the real reason it wasn't as good as I would have liked? To be honest speed has a lot to do with everything.

You are always multi-tasking, when things go wrong it's like your brain being over overloaded and like a computer it will freeze or crash on you, but if you slowed down and did manageable things over a longer period, then you may find that you are reading the road ahead a lot further, and making better decisions, allowing your skills to go from conscious to sub-conscious skills.

To gain the very best out of learning, you need to be relaxed and happy!

To take full responsibility from day one for all your actions. Focus on the moment, dealing with each individual scenario and giving yourselves praise when you manage to achieve small mile stones.

Don't carry excess mental baggage with you, for example:

- An argument with partner.
- Being late to start or finish
- Traffic in front or behind being annoying
- You must pass your test!
- What if I fail…
- What if I make a mistake?

None of the above have anything to do with your ability to drive the car. Your mind set is the only thing that will ever dictate how well you drive. It's how you perceive things, if you imagine there are 2 worlds, your inner world and the outside world. In the outside world people only see what you show them, a reflection of your inner world.

Like a mirror, in the outside world there is no fear, happiness, love, hate etc, only what you bring to the outside world is what is seen. For example, there is an empty room next door, it has no energy, no atmosphere, just a room, then you and 10 friends turn up who you haven't seen for years. There would be good, positive vibrations in that room now. If it was a wake, and there was just you, that room would be sad, depressed, cold… but it is still the same room, things only change when you bring something from within into the outside world, into the room next door….

GIVING UP YOUR RIGHT TO DRIVE

HELP – DON'T HINDER

GIVING UP YOUR RIGHT TO DRIVE

You have the ultimate power to choose what you reflect, or bring into that room next door. That room next door could be a job interview, a driving test, an exam, anything at all! What do you want to bring?

How do you want people to see you, what can you contribute or offer or see who you are? Fear does play a massive part of an inexperienced mind, but let's look at that list above again.

And let's take the driving test, what fear factors and negative thoughts enter our mind?

- What if I make a mistake?
- What if the car doesn't start?
- What if the examiner is harsh?
- What if the examiner doesn't like me?

I see a lot of what ifs…. this is where you need to change your mind set to what if I drive well etc.…

I had a pupil not so long ago say to me "Mark what if the car won't start?" I said a good way to control these negative thoughts was to simply blow them out of context.

The example I gave to this true event was "you're right the car might not start, the engine might fall out, oil is leaking everywhere, the oil has reached the building behind us and then a member of the public throws a cigarette down and then the oil catches alight, and then the building goes up in flames and then people are jumping out of office windows and then……

By this time your brain says: how ridiculous, people aren't jumping out of windows, the building's not on fire, there is no oil leak, the engine hasn't fallen out, there's nothing wrong at all. You are reprogramming your brain to learn to curve these "what ifs" for you to learn reality. To condition your mind on the facts!

The fact is:

- You are there to carry out an assessment to gain your licence to drive a car, set by the DVSA
- The car you are using is at the required standard in its type and current condition
- The examiners are trained to be emotionally detached and are only able to record faults
- You have already demonstrated to your instructor you have gained the ability to drive unaided to a very satisfactory level of confidence

Then you have the HOPE factor:

- I hope I pass
- I hope I make you proud
- I hope it's easy
- I hope it's not raining

HELP – DON'T HINDER

GIVING UP YOUR RIGHT TO DRIVE

"Hope" is a delusion. Hope does not exist. Having faith does!

We use the word hope for far too much, this word can only lead you to disappointment. Because your test may not be easy, could well be raining, you may not pass, and the instructor may not be proud. But if you have FAITH...

- I will pass my test; I believe in my ability.
- I will give 100% of my ability which I know will make you and me proud!
- The test will be as easy as I make it!
- The weather will not phase me as I have driven at all different times and have no control over the weather.

A complete new mind set has already granted you confidence and the right attitude and the right mirror image you want to project to the person or situation you wish, empowering you to the best you can be.

Don't get me wrong you still may fail this test, as your own perception may differ from the examiners, but at least you haven't failed yourself!

If you give a 100% on everything you do you will always be a winner, just sometimes it doesn't always feel like that.

Take what the examiner has fed back to you, take his comments constructively, take responsibility for the faults, why and how did they happen?

The examiner has experience and can see where these faults may end up if unidentified with your best interests and others at heart.

It is very often when a pupil fails a test they can't see why, or they can't remember the mistake, until their mind is calm and they look back and say "yes, I understand that now and I have since put it right!"

Remember driving is a life skill, it does take time to develop, everybody learns at different speeds, don't put pressure onto yourself like I must pass I have a new job next week, I need my licence. Or I better pass 1st time because my mum did, or I'm giving up if I don't pass because it's embarrassing etc....

You will pass when you are ready to! That's it! But having the best mindset will certainly help not just for this but all life's encounters.

Ladies as a man we men are often on the end of your PMT week.

I know we laugh and joke but on a serious note some of you do find that in your body's cycle you aren't always able to focus at your best, so book your tests away from these times, when everything falls into your best alignment.

The Theory Test

Before you can apply for the practical test you must obtain a pass in the theory test, you then use your pass certificate number when booking your practical test of ability. This has been problematic for some pupils, especially if they have learning difficulties or learning disabilities.

To be fair, there are measures in place to help pupils who generally struggle with this kind of test, if notified in advance with supporting evidence the DVSA (through Pearsons) allow more time and if required a voice over which reads the questions out on behalf of the reader.

Back in 2016 – 2018 I decided to open up a workshop, running my very own classes for such pupils, I called it **TU** short for **Theory Uncovered**, over 5 weeks and totalling around 10-12 hours, I had a good classroom of 10 – 20 pupils turning up for this condensed and informative bespoke course. Now I say bespoke because I had a definite purpose, to get the unknown to become known in pupils' minds, and I achieved this by not just going through questions but physically breaking the questions down and exploring the answers.

Now at this stage the average pupil had already failed their theory test a good 4-5 times and were desperate.

By the time my course finished each person that took their theory test passed with 100% results and this gave me the confidence to run another course, and then another. The feedback I received was incredible, I mean designing a course, finding a suitable location and actually delivering the course with no previous experience was a massive feat, and to actually charge a fee and get results was amazing too, unfortunately whilst I really enjoyed running this course I wasn't getting the number of pupils in. Yes, there was a demand for my course but people couldn't drive to get there, or the days or times for the course may not have been convenient, so at this point in time I am working with an idea that's under construction to reach the whole of the UK from their very own living rooms. Whilst that's something coming in the future, let's look at how I can help right here and now!

So in short what I discovered over a period of time was this, pupils were failing their theory test partly due to the following:

- Forgot the test day or time.
- Didn't take licence with them.
- Got flustered before turning up such as transport letting them down or just forgot where they put their documentation.
- Rushed the test.
- Didn't read the question properly.
- Had not put enough time in to revise.
- Missed hidden clues or prompts.
- Human error.

HELP – DON'T HINDER

THE THEORY TEST

THE THEORY TEST

So to pass the theory test you need at least 44/50 to pass and then go onto the 2nd part which is the hazard perception test.

So don't lace your chances of failure, set all documentation out the night before so you know exactly where everything is, and have transportation organised with a back up plan!

Be there at least 15 minutes beforehand, calm and collected.

Now if you want to pass you shouldn't just wing it. Complete the apps you have been training with, I personally recommend the DVSA OFFICIAL TEST KIT. I would seriously recommend reading every question in each section and taking the trouble of actually understanding it! The app is really well put together with the Highway Code and explanation on everything required.

TIP: do not speed read the questions, read it twice, you have more time than you think.

Sometimes the answer is in the question, for example:

> **When would you use a multi-occupants lane?**
> A When you're late
> B When you're tired
> C In heavy traffic
> D When there are two or more **occupants**

As you can see I have highlighted D because it has the word occupants in it.

Take away the answers you know to be wrong (the science of deductions) and if you're left with a 50/50 choice then always go for the **safest** answer.

TIP: You can also flag questions and return to them at the end of the test, this way you won't feel rushed from spending too much time on questions you are not so confident about.

Try to remember back to a real situation where you can recall what a parent or friend had done whilst they were driving.

But my favourite and probably the best advice I can give you is this, read the question, understand the question, then think of the answer before looking at their answers, now if you have a answer in your mind and you then see that answer displayed then go for it! This will help you from doubting yourself or changing your mind and will boost your confidence. But please don't put massive pressure on yourself if you don't pass, it can be done again and again, I believe there are apps on the market that when booking your theory test you can have unlimited tests.

The importance of all of this is to ensure you as a driver understand to a good standard what things mean and where and when to apply them.

THE THEORY TEST

HAZARD PERCEPTION TEST

The second part of your theory test is to demonstrate your recognition of a developing hazard.

At the time of my publishing this article you would see on the computer screen a stationary clip with a 10 second count down.

TIP: Use that 10 second clip to see the environment you will be starting on!
This can be very useful once you have read through what has been written below.

Once the count down has finished the screen will give you the perception as if you were driving the car along a road, on 13 clips there will be 1 developing hazard and on 1 other clip there will be 2 hazards, now this could come up on your 1st clip yet it could be your 14th clip?

What I advised my pupils to do was break the potential clips into categories for example:

- Countryside
- Dual carriageway / motorways
- Town centre
- Urban estate

Then I would suggest on paper write down all potential hazards for each category you can think of. So for countryside it could look like this:

- Cattle on road
- Horses
- Walkers
- Joggers
- Fallen trees
- Large puddles
- Fresh mud off fields

Now because you have inscribed in your mind the list you have just made, watch the hazard clips on countryside and see how many you spotted, and any hazards that you didn't think of add them to your list!

When it comes to your real test the hazard should stick out! And if you do this with the other areas like town or urban it would make the test so much easier especially with the scorings, as if you spot the hazard developing too late then this would effect your marks.

The score starts at 5 then runs down 4,3,2,1 and 0, you will also score 0 if you click too many times as the computer will assume you are trying to trick it, so the computer is only expecting you to click on a developing hazard, once or twice.

TIP: Practise on as many clips as possible there are many cheap or even free practice clips on the web.

THE THEORY TEST

THE TEST

The Test

When it comes to the driving test, many things lace your chances of passing and probably 99% are all from inside your mind! Yes it's hardly ever just rotten luck, or the examiners were mean, or simply didn't like you, no lets look at a more reasonable and realistic point of view.

Before we start, take a moment to think about two factors:

1) The word perception
2) Risk assessment.

Perception is not just the way you see something but it's also got to be the way your Examiner does too! So in theory you should both read the driving in the same way and that should be read from my 2nd point – risk assessment.

Now the way I see this is quite a simple aspect: when there's an accident, the accident didn't just happen, like any crisis there's a build up from bad decisions, every action has a reaction and the bad decision will lead to another bad decision until you've gone down the wrong path of thought impairing good conscious decisions.

A driver driving down a straight road at a suitable speed shouldn't cause a high risk, risk level is low.

Now place a parked car on the same road and as the driver approaches the parked car and unless he/she changes their driving behavior, there could be an issue as risk is becoming higher. So, if the driver checks their mirrors to ensure safe overtaking and signals to inform others of their intention, slows the car down and changes gear down allowing for potential danger of doors opening or people stepping out, they have automatically taken a real positive step in the reduction of the potential risk becoming higher.

Now you can see this clearly from 2 points of view:

1) The learner could say: "It wasn't my fault the door opened, I couldn't see if anyone was in the car, they should have checked before they opened the door!"

2) The Examiner's point of view: "It wasn't the door opening, that caused us to swerve into on coming cars, that caused a failure, it was the fact that your driving behaviour hadn't changed and you didn't respond in advance, allowing the correct speed or room on the approach to lower the risk that got you a failure!"

So the same situation has two very different takes on the test.

So in short when the driving risk starts to get greater the driving behaviour needs to adjust in such a way that the risk lowers as soon as possible from either slowing down creating more time for you and on coming cars to adjust or changing direction to cater for the "WHAT IF" scenario to come into full force.

THE TEST

Let's look at what else could lace your chances of passing:

1) Fear - fear of failing, fear of passing and being left on your own, fear of tests, fear of making mistakes, fear of letting people other than yourself down, fear of causing traffic to get angry, fear of accidents, the word FEAR plays a massive part which I will come back to shortly.

2) Not being ready - not learning to a confident level across the full spectrum of driving modules.

3) Missing tests - not being organised, thinking test is tomorrow when it was today, personal organisation, having everything you need like your licence with you and any other paperwork required, will certainly stop unnecessary panicking. I've had pupils book the wrong Test Centre and parents have booked it under the wrong name. Pupils turn up with the incorrect money to pay the instructor not realizing the instructor needs paying for the car on test as they cannot teach a lesson whilst you are using their car for the test and the instructor has refused to take them out! This has not happened with me but I have seen it happen.

4) Not believing in one's self - you've covered all the areas with your chosen instructor and should be ready but the person who says they can pass is usually correct but the person that says they can't pass is also usually correct. It is self belief.

5) Rushing the test - wanting it to be over as quickly as possible, this mindset can lead you into driving too fast for you, whilst you may not break speed limits you may drive without the due care and attention that you need for that particular scenario, causing minor or serious faults!

After all the test will take approximately 40-45 minutes just because you got round the route in 30 minutes you may find you hadn't allowed time for really effective observation or allow the correct driving attitude towards others etc and thus fail.

These are only some of the many reasons you can lace your own test resulting in dooming your potential.

On the flip side, and more positive side, there are habits or rituals that you can do to improve your chances of passing. Here below is a small list of proven methods my own pupils have experienced:

1) Self confidence - without being over confident

2) Clarity on your task ahead

3) Being calm and relaxed

4) Visualise leading up to test passing 1st time

5) Knowing in yourself what gives you focus - for some pupils being angry gives them focus

6) Extraction of fear of failure and the "what if" scenario as mentioned earlier in this book.

7) Don't tell everyone you have the test, as this could trigger excess pressure

8) Have at least 1-2 hours driving before test, to help get you in the driving mindset

9) People who suffer with anxiety may use Rescue Remedy or calming tablets, or even beta blockers, but you must seek medical professional advice before taking medications. Pupils have even had hypnosis leading up to tests, bottom line is choose what works for you, as everyone is different and acts differently to different stresses.

THE TEST

HELP – DON'T HINDER

THE TEST

10) Looking at the test from a different perspective, like imagine you have already passed the dreaded test and you are working as a taxi driver for friend, and don't worry the person you're picking up knows the way he will tell you exactly where to go!

At the end of the day the reality of this so called test is, it's only an assessment which can be taken as many times as is needed, you don't have control of the:

Traffic

Route

Examiner

So there's no point in worrying about any of the above, just focus on what you do have control over, and that's what you've been working towards with your chosen mentor - yep, simply drive the car as you see fit. If you drive true to yourself any faults will be highlighted for your own safety and the welfare of the general public which is what you really want deep down, and when you pass you will not only have the belief of the instructor but also have beliefs of the examiner and this should boost your own self confidence.

So by understanding the Driving Test Report DL25A as shown, it should help pupils parents and instructors:

Let's break it down:

1a: Eye sight test - you must be able to read a number plate from 67.9 feet , ensure if you wear glasses or contact lenses then you must wear them whilst you drive, if you fail the eye sight test twice the examiner will come back with a tape measure and physically measure this distance, if still incorrect then the test won't go ahead. You may also wear sunglasses no problem but remember to make sure the examiners can see you checking mirrors, etc as they can't see your eyes so make it more obvious that you are observing clearly.

1b: If you're taking a specialised test such as tractor test then at the end of this test you would be asked a Highway Code question and to identify road signs

If it was a LGV/ PCV then these questions would be on things like location and operations of safety components like fire extinguishers or fuel cut-off switch's and emergency exits etc.

2: Controlled stop - otherwise known as emergency stop, as covered earlier in the book, the examiner is checking that you have stopped the car as quickly as possible whilst staying in full control, just remember in wet or icy conditions it could take you longer to stop than normal, once you have made the vehicle safe moving off safely is equally as important! Check left and right shoulders and only move off once safe to do so.

3,4,5,6 are the manoeuvres.

Since 4th Dec 2017 the reverse around the left corner and turn in the road has been replaced with bay parking, pull up on the right reverse exercise.

In short whichever exercise you have make sure you stay in full control and are taking effective observations throughout the exercise acting on what you see!

Driving Test Report

DL25A
0408

I declare that:
- the use of the test vehicle for the purposes of the test is fully covered by a valid policy of insurance which satisfies the requirements of the relevant legislation.
- I normally live/have lived in the UK for at least 185 days in the last 12 months (except taxi/private hire). See note 30.

S / D/C

Application Ref.
Date / Time / Dr./No.
DTC Code / Authority / Reg. No.
Staff / Ref. No.

Cat. Type / Auto / Ext
Instructor Reg
Instructor Cert / Sup / ADI / Int / Other / C

	Total S D		Total S D		Total S D
1a Eyesight		13 Move off — safety		23 Positioning — normal driving	
1b H/Code / Safety		control		lane discipline	
2 Controlled Stop		14 Use of mirrors- M/C rear obs — signalling		24 Pedestrian crossings	
		change direction		25 Position / normal stops	
3 Reverse / Left Reverse with trailer — control		change speed		26 Awareness / planning	
observation		15 Signals — necessary		27 Ancillary controls	
4 Reverse / Right — control		correctly		28 Spare 1	
observation		timed		29 Spare 2	
5 Reverse Park — control		16 Clearance / obstructions		30 Spare 3	
R C obs.		17 Response to signs / signals — traffic signs		31 Spare 4	
6 Turn in road — control		road markings		32 Spare 5	
observation		traffic lights		33 Wheelchair Pass Fail	
7 Vehicle checks		traffic controllers		Pass Fail None	Total Faults Route No.
8 Forward park / Taxi manoeuvre — control		other road users			
observation		18 Use of speed		ETA V P D255	
9 Taxi wheelchair		19 Following distance		Survey A B C D	
10 Uncouple / recouple		20 Progress — appropriate speed		E F G H	
11 Precautions		undue hesitation		Eco Safe driving — Control	
12 Control — accelerator		21 Junctions — approach speed		Planning	
clutch		observation		Debrief Activity Code	
gears		turning right		I acknowledge receipt of Pass Certificate Number:	Licence rec'd Yes
footbrake		turning left		Wheelchair Cert. No:	COA
parking brake / MC front brake		cutting corners			No
steering		22 Judgement — overtaking		There has been no change to my health: see note 29 overleaf.	
balance M/C		meeting			
PCV door exercise		crossing			

© Crown Copyright 12/2017

DVSA – An executive agency of the Department for Transport

Form Ref. DL25 D0018000-00

HELP – DON'T HINDER

THE TEST

7 vehicle checks – this is the show me / tell me exercise.

1 of 14 questions will be asked at the start of your test and whilst on the move, these can be found on the government website by googling DVSA show me tell me questions.

Which I will also show below, but be aware these questions can change so whilst you're reading my book please be aware to double check leading up to your test.

(Current as of 2nd April 2019).

- **Tell me how you'd check that the brakes are working before starting a journey.**
  Brakes should not feel spongy or slack, brakes should be tested as you set off and the car shouldn't pull to one side. (What they mean by spongy is imagine a sponge that's wet, if you squeezed it and let go it would take awhile for it to recalibrate back to its original position.)

- **Tell me where you'd find the information for the recommended tyre pressure for this car and how tyre pressure should be checked.**
  Manufacturer's guide, use a reliable pressure gauge, check and adjust when tyres are cold not forgetting the spare wheel. Replace all caps. In most cars there's normally a plaque on the inside of the door jams or sills in door well that will also show ideal pressures for front and rear tyres as well as car load types. The tyre pressure written on the side of the tyre are normally maximum pressure only which you would normally drive on.

- **Tell me how you make sure your head restraint is correctly adjusted so it provides the best protection in the event of a crash.**
  The head restraint should be adjusted so the rigid part of the restraint is at least as high as the eye or top of the ears, and is as close to the back of the head as is comfortable. Some restraints might not be adjustable.

- **Tell me how you'd check the tyres have sufficient tread and depth and that their general condition is safe to use on the road.**
  No cut's or bulges (or any damage) to the outside wall that could cause the tyre to burst and the tyre has 1.6mm of tread depth across the central three-quarters (75%) of the breadth of the tyre and around the entire circumference of the tyre. You could use a tyre depth gauge, or 20p piece to measure quick and easy, but most tyre fitters are normally happy to check free of charge for you.

- **Tell me how you would check that the headlights and tail lights are working.**
  Explain you'd operate the switch (turning ignition on if required) then walk around vehicle. (Remember this is a tell me question so no need to physically walk round).

- **Tell me how you'd know if there was a problem with the anti-lock braking system.**
  Warning light should illuminate if there is a fault. Most displays would show ABS light up.

- **Tell me how you'd check the directional indicators are working.**

THE TEST

HELP – DON'T HINDER

Explain you'd operate the switch (with ignition on if required) and walk round the vehicle, as this is a tell me question you don't need to physically walk round. You could also put on your hazard lights to see all bulbs working for indicators or with cars that have a key fob to lock vehicles this too can flash your lights!

- **Tell me how you'd check your brake lights are working on this car.**
  You would reverse up to a reflective surface, glass windows, walls, etc, and operate the foot brake making full use of the reflections or ask someone to help (ideally this should be done at least once a week or before a long journey)

- **Tell me how you'd check the powered assisted steering is working before starting a journey.**
  Start the car up and steering should feel light, with a little pressure on the wheel whilst starting you may feel the steering judder as it activates.

- **Tell me how you'd switch on the rear fog light(s) and explain when you'd use them/it. You don't need to exit the vehicle.**
  Operate the dipped headlights with ignition on if required, then switch fog light(s) on. You should see illumination of the warning light showing its active. You should put the fog light(s) on when visibility is seriously reduced to less than 100 meters.

- **Tell me how you'd switch your headlight from dipped beam to main beam and explain how you'd know the main beam is on.**
  Operate the switch (with ignition/engine on if required) and check main beam warning light is on. This is when the green dipped lights warning light goes to a blue warning light.

The next 3 questions they could ask are opening the bonnet of your vehicle to tell them how you'd check for sufficient levels of either:

- **Oil** – locate dip stick, take out, wipe replace and take back out again and look at min/max reading, do this when engine is cold and on a flat surface to ensure accurate reading at least once a week or before a long journey. If oil needs to be topped up place in small amounts (say ½ pint) at a time and allow to settle before topping up again.

- **Coolant** – locate coolant tank look for min/max line, if low when car is cold unscrew filler cap and top up with coolant to required level. Don't do this if engine is hot as you may get scalded from steam when removing cap.

- **Hydraulic brake fluid** – this is normally checked yearly on MOT, servicing, etc, by the garage however by finding the brake fluid tank this also has a min/max mark and if you have any concerns you can top up yourself or take it to local garage.

TIP – also check windscreen wash once a week or before a long journey. It is a legal requirement for your car to have windscreen wash and you could even fail an MOT if it's empty.

So these are the current list of tell me questions which is designed for all drivers to have some very basic knowledge on safety checks or good practice drills to avoid any unforeseen problems which may of not been picked up by instructors or have been forgotten by pupils!

My first lesson plan I do for pupils is normally a controls lesson explaining in detail where everything is and how it works but if a pupil has had say 30 hours of tuition during the day time there's a real chance they've forgotten where the lights are, or even how to switch them on! And because of this factor pupils who pass in your car and drive there own then get distracted whilst messing around looking for switches dials or buttons to press taking away there concentration from the road thus causing a accident.

With this said the DVSA realised this was important to assess the pupils ability to be able to operate controls on the move, safely, without altering their course, or direction, or speed, so number 27 on the driving test report is marked ancillary controls. This would be where you may find a minor, serious, or dangerous fault if you operated an ancillary control without care and attention.

Below I've created a list of things the examiner will ask you to complete whilst on the drive, even though they will only ask you one there may be times that naturally you would have to do more to suit weather conditions. In all the cases listed below the ancillaries should be switched on when safe to do so

1) **Wash / clean rear window**
2) **Wash / clean front window**
3) **Switch on dipped head lights**
4) **Set rear demister**
5) **Operate the horn**
6) **Demist front window**
7) **Open/close side window**

8) **You could also become confident in:**

- Switch fog lights on
- Air con on
- Air circulation on
- Hazard lights on/off
- Dipped to full beam

9) **NUMBER 9 on the DL25A form** is a manoeuvre for the taxi test followed up with the taxi driver showing his ability to collapse and fold up a wheelchair and store in car securely.

10) UNCOUPLE/ RECOUPLE

This is for the trailer test only, showing you can hook up the trailer and disconnect safely. Making effective use of the stabiliser if fitted, breakaway cable and correct use of the jockey wheel.

11) PRECAUTIONS

Whenever you are making the vehicle safe when stopping you are required to place hand brake followed by neutral gear. If you were to stop and select neutral but didn't find the neutral gear and bring clutch up

THE TEST

the vehicle could well shoot forwards/ backwards depending on the gear selected potentially causing an accident. So, by making the same mistake but applying the handbrake first would eliminate the movement of the vehicle considerably avoiding possible accident, so the examiners would like to see handbrake/neutral every time you are stopping the car to park up.

12) CONTROLS

Under this part of the form the examiners are looking for your ability, understanding and control of the following controls:

Accelerator – under no circumstances should you rev the engine more than needed.

For example, common mistakes I've found pupils make for this are leaving foot on the accelerator peddle whilst changing gear, more so on fast roads like dual carriageways as their foot is further down on the gas pedal than normally around town. There should be no revving to try and rush or intimidate pedestrian's crossing the road, or in my experience feeding the engine to much fuel to get up hills, whilst you may require more power to go up steep hills from moving off it should be noted use enough not excessive!

Clutch – the examiner is looking at the use of your clutch, ensuring you depress the clutch fully for selecting your desired gear or for good clutch control whilst manoeuvring the car slow in controlled area's such as around parked vehicles or peeping and creeping out of tight junctions etc.

Gears – selecting the correct gear for the speed you are doing, common mistakes that pupils make are whilst they are carrying out their mirror-signal-manoeuvre routine they should also focus on position-speed-gear-look and more often than not they misjudge and bring their speed down but feel they run out of time to then change down not just in town traffic but junctions and roundabouts, thus causing them to stall.

I try to instil in their minds, slow down, change down, speed up, change up.

Foot brake – there should be no unnecessary sharp braking, now don't mistake unnecessary braking! Whilst the pupil forward plans the level of risk and shows good knowledge on when to adjust their driving behaviour to suit conditions there will be situations that may be unforeseen and require firmer braking.

Common mistakes seem to occur more when the pupil reacts very late to a developing hazard due to poor planning or observation and due to reacting late causing sharp and therefore unnecessary braking, this is where most of the time the pupil would say "crumbs, he pulled out on me" of which the examiner might be thinking" crumbs this pupil should be easing off here because of potential unforeseen danger".

Parking brake/MC front brake - when applying the hand brake apply on full, and release fully when required, make sure you know your limits when applying this don't put it on so hard you can't get it off!

Put the hand brake on when stationary for long periods of time, or if you're on a hill, I also would personally recommend you put the hand brake on when you come to a stop sign, to show examiner your vehicle has come to a complete stop.

From experience if you attempt to take off the hand brake but its not all the way down and it beeps and you then release it the rest of the way the examiner normally overlooks this, but wont overlook it if you haven't attempted to take it off and try and drive with it on.

THE TEST

Steering – you should show you have great steering control, using both hands to feed the steering wheel round with both hands maintaining a good road position, don't let the steering wheel spin through your hands or anything where potentially you could lose control, at slow speeds whilst reversing you could steer with one hand or cross arms if required as the car is controlled and slow.

You would more than likely get marked down for brushing or striking kerbs or swerving unnecessarily and not staying in your designated lane.

Balance – this is the balance between gas, brake and clutch. If you didn't have good balance with these controls, then situations like stalling the car or kangarooing (i.e. jerking the car forwards or backwards) or over-revving the engine would normally be the result and would be deemed as a fault. To find a good balance you ideally want to have your bite point (when the clutch plates make first contact and you can hear the tone of the engine change) and then to come off either of the brakes and apply the correct pressure to the accelerator for the car to move smoothly at the desired speed required.

As you can appreciate sometimes moving the car around corners or other vehicles would need to be done slowly and gently, other times you may need to get away quickly at a round-a-bout in either or any situation you have to show that you have the right balance.

TIP: to help pupils find this balance I make up a random story and it goes something like this:

Imagine there is a elephant in front of the car facing away from you, and we tie a piece of cotton to its tail and connect the other end of the cotton to the front of your car. You can control the elephants movements by bringing up the clutch pedal, if you bring it up slowly it's like whispering in the elephants ear "walk on" so as the elephant walks forward the cotton gets tighter and as you feel the tension come off the brake and with a little luck the cotton won't break and the car may move!

Now cotton is a little week, if we wanted to make the cotton into chain which pedal could do this? Most of the pupil's would quite rightly say the gas/accelerator pedal, "sure" I would say and then suggest if we whacked the elephant on its backside he would run off and as the chain won't snap then sure enough we would go with him. However, we don't really want chain all the time as this could be an overkill, perhaps a lump of rope would be a much better compromise!

The pupils soon work out what cotton, rope and chain sounds like as well as hearing the difference.

13) MOVING OFF

Safely: You must show that you can move off in various situations using full effect use of observation without causing any other road users to slow down, change direction or take evasive action. This can include moving off from either side of the road, on a hill or an angle start when required to do so.

Under control: You should try not to stall the car; wheel spin the car or roll back.

14) USE OF MIRRORS

When signalling: The examiner is watching you to ensure you have taken the correct and effective use of your mirror checks. (Checking your mirrors before you signal doesn't make it effective unless you physically act on what you see! For arguments sake if you're pulling over to park and nobody was around, then a signal

HELP – DON'T HINDER

THE TEST

HELP – DON'T HINDER

wouldn't be required, so there must be a conscious decision based on what you observe.

When changing direction: Before you move your car either left or right whether to overtake change lanes or turn, you must take effective use of these mirrors, your rear view mirror first, followed by either the left or right exterior mirror depending on the direction you choose to go. Please remember if turning left or right at a junction then a signal should always follow.

When changing speed: Before you speed up or slow down you should have taken effective use of your rear view mirror.

However I really think you should raise the question to why? Telling a new driver just to do it will probably go in one ear and out the other, throughout all my training I always try and incorporate client centred learning, so ask the pupil why? Why should you check the rear view mirror before speeding up or slowing down? Prompt him by saying "why is it so important to check your mirror before slowing or what impact could you slowing have on the following vehicles ? if the car behind was really close when you looked in your rear view mirror how would you act when you come to slow down or stop?

Then the same Q & A When speeding up. The real important lesson here like everything else I teach is to make a real link, a reason for doing anything. Then when pupils make that conscious decision, they will know when, why and how to do it sub-consciously, at the right time for the right reasons, not just getting fed up with you moaning saying "MIRRORS" every five minutes.

15) SIGNALS

Necessary: You are to show the examiner clearly when a signal is necessary and when not, as like your mirrors above, signals should be placed on a conscious decision not as a matter of routine.

Correctly: If a signal cancels itself, reapply. Don't signal left if your turning right! (Tip: if you did signal the wrong way by mistake, then go the way you have signalled, the examiner will get you back on course!)

Timed: Make sure you signal at the right time, identify the road or direction you plan to take and then signal.

If you signal too early then other road users will think you may be doing something different, signal too late and other road users won't be able to process what your intentions are in time and potentially be on course for a collision.

Sometimes there could be two or three roads close together and the examiner may say take your third road on the right, so in this instance you may be able to apply a signal before the road you wish, as the warning to other road users outweighs the normal protocol for turning and therefore deemed safer.

16) CLEARANCE OF OBSTRUCTIONS

Throughout your drive you should have shown that you recognize through your actions to leave adequate clearance to parked cars; cyclists; horse riders and larger vehicles such as lorries and buses due to the associated hazards. So when passing cars you should be no less than 1 metre (4 feet or a doors width). Cyclists and horses are more vulnerable so approx 6 feet clearance.

Now the examiner will recognise that the road may have cars or vehicles either side and be somewhat more narrow, however as this situation starts to become more hazardous the pupil must also show by adapting their driving behaviour to suit these situations and the best way from my experience is to reduce their speed in kind, slow right down, change gears down so they have time to react safely to any situation that may arise.

Looking ahead and planning well in advance will certainly help, be extra cautious around work vehicles and buses as visibility may be more restricted than normal as well as the time of day, for example schools starting or finishing, busy periods such as rush hour, but also drive intelligently, at night time you may wish to drive wider when going past groups of people on narrow paths, especially if they have just come from a pub or night club etc.

17) RESPONSE TO SIGNS & SIGNALS

In this section on the driving test report the examiner is assessing the driver for their response to:

Traffic signs: Look for and act on all traffic signs, they have been placed there to advise or help you to make the right driving decisions, if you miss these signs you may make speeding faults or fall into a harbour, it's the drivers responsibility to act on what they see. However I'm sure the examiner will soon let you know if it's anything too bad, as I'm sure they wouldn't wish to fly off a cliff with you.

Road markings: Again respond to what you see, they are placed strategically to advise and help you.

Traffic lights: Anticipate when lights are likely to change, forward planning and awareness will aid you in having a smooth drive.

Traffic controllers: This is where you would respond to Police or highways staff directing you in case of road works, accidents etc.

The examiner is watching to see how you react to there arm signals or communication and assessing your ability to act on what you see.

And other road users: Again seeing how you respond to other drivers or road users. Act on what you see.

TIP: Whilst you may be beckoned on, don't beckon others by waving hands or flashing lights! You should only use hand signals as per the highway code.

18) USE OF SPEED

You should aim to drive at the speed of the road taking into account the road, weather and traffic conditions at a speed that you can see and stop within.

The examiner will look to see if your judgement is good and are confident in your drive.

19) FOLLOWING DISTANCE

Whilst you are driving you are constantly observing how the risks are increasing along your journey and unless you adapt your driving behaviour to the road context the risks become greater.

From my own experience one of the contributing risks is how close you are to the vehicle ahead, so the examination board want to see that when you stop in traffic you should be able to see the two T's "tyres to tarmac" so you can visible see the vehicles back tyres touching the road.

The advantages of this is the following:
If the vehicle in front rolls back, you could beep your horn or take evasive action.
If the vehicle breaks down, you should have enough room to get around.
Would have clearer visibility to see further ahead.

Driving around town you should have at least two car lengths of clearance in slow moving traffic to allow time to stop if needed and on faster moving roads at least using the 2 second rule in dry weather (good conditions) 4 second rule on wet surfaces, and 20 second rule (x10 of the normal 2 second rule) for adverse conditions such as sleet snow and ice.

The way to calculate this rule is by simply seeing the vehicle in front go past something solid like a signpost or tree and count these seconds before you go through the same point.

If you neglect these points you may be doomed for failure.

TIP: Watch out for vehicle over taking you and coming back early, it is your responsibility to drop back!

Also, if you overtake allow correct distance before returning.

20) PROGRESS

Appropriate speed: whilst continuously evaluating your driving risk, you are required to drive in a confident manner approaching hazards at a safe speed without going to slow, so being realistic to the environment you're in.

Don't drive too slow as this can frustrate other road users and could cause unnecessary danger to yourself and others. Try and be in a situation where you could approach a junction and be ready to go at the first safe opportunity. And when you do go, increase to the speed of the road, traffic and weather conditions.

Remember when approaching T-junctions you have the two types – open and closed. By taking early good observation you should be able to maintain a fluent motion, and closed junctions try and focus more on going down to 1st gear on the approach, steering round to stay in line with your curb and then whilst about to pause, lean forward and have a really good look up and down the road and then act on what you see.

Pupils do seem like they either forget to change gear at this point and stall because of gear fault, or they end up wide especially turning left, or they come to a complete stop, changing gear and then when they get a chance to go they have missed the opportunity and miss the concept of undue hesitancy.

21) JUNCTIONS

Approach speed: You could get marked down in this area if you drove too fast and required strong braking to stop at the end of the road. Like wise they don't want you dribbling up to the end of the road holding other traffic up.

Pull up to the junction where you're in a great position to be able to go or pause, ensuring you don't stop over the line or too short of the line.

Observation: you must take effective observation, it's far better to take a real good clear look up and down the road so in your mind your decision to go is crystal than to look fast and assume it's all good.

THE TEST

Special awareness should be taken when obstructions are present like parked vehicles. Feel free to peep and creep forwards without over committing to enable to make a more educated decision before pulling out, especially smaller vehicles like mobility scooters or motorbikes.

But also remember the time of year! Yes the time of year could change your visibility, for example for 9 months of the year you approach a mini roundabout, and can see on the approach every day, but what happens is vegetation starts growing especially in the summer and people start driving their sports cars, much lower and faster and can easily be hidden. Note: no situation is ever the same!

Turning right: when turning right you must position your car in the correct position. On a one way street well to the right, when turning out of a tight road stay well to the left to create more space, on a wide road position just to the left of the central reservation line to allow following cars to come past on the left, not to cause unnecessary congestion.

If turning right into the road then focus on steering at your point of turn if clear to do so or be prepared to pause just before your point of turn if waiting. Just make sure you keep your wheels straight whilst paused in case of a collision from the rear. You don't want to be pushed into the path of oncoming vehicles!

Turning left: if it's a sharp corner ensure your speed is at a suitable speed for you to be able to get your steering on and off comfortably without going off at a tangent, but also at a speed you can steer at your point of turn. If it's a sweeping corner or long corner then go around with the curb, staying reasonably close.

Whilst you're approaching your turn, remember your actions are a signal to other road users. If you approach way too fast people may not think you are turning and they may not respond as you think they would.

This can be potentially dangerous.

Cutting corners: turning too early into a road means you are cutting corners, driving on the wrong side of the road, making the road too narrow for on coming vehicles, you may also find that you haven't been able to take full advantage of observation, often leading to dangerous faults.

22) JUDGEMENT

Overtaking: On your test situations may arise for you to overtake, make sure it's safe and legal to do so. Allow good time to execute this, make sure its viable, i.e. you may have a bend ahead and you don't really want to come into the bend faster than you would normally want, don't drive on the wrong side of the road longer than necessary.

Whilst overtaking horses or cyclists allow a good 6-foot (1.5 meters) clearance and parked vehicles 4 feet (1 meter) giving correct mirror checks and signals. If you can't give these distances due to the road being tighter then either reduce speed and gears to deal with the risks involved or hold back until a safer opportunity prevails, remember driving is a privilege not a priority.

Meeting: When meeting other traffic make sure you clearly understand what the other road users' intentions are. Give plenty of clearance and give way when required, don't just follow the last vehicle through, make your own conscious decision.

Crossing traffic: Do not turn in front of oncoming traffic unless it is safe to do so.

THE TEST

23) POSITIONING

Normal driving position: your position can be judged as a signal, so, always drive to the left of your lane, (approx. 2 feet from the curb)

Stay clear of parked vehicles and read the road for markings signs and signals. Try to avoid potholes where possible and large puddles.

Lane disciplines: you need to be able to follow and act on all road and lane markings in good time, as other people could interpret your position as a signal and may start to adapt a new road position before or quicker than you. Be aware of your position always and those around you. Remember any change in direction consult appropriate mirrors in advance.

24) PEDESTRIAN CROSSINGS

Now bearing in mind there are at least five different types of pedestrian crossings you need to think about the one you are approaching. As you can appreciate if you can anticipate the crossing early on then your action would normally be a correct one! For example if you approached a pelican crossing and there were people waiting to cross then there would be no surprise that the amber light would show thus going to red, if you had checked your mirror and eased off your accelerator you are showing in advance that you are preparing to stop, meaning not only have you seen the crossing but you are also reducing the risk of harsh braking last minute, and being able to pause at the right place, without stressing the drivers behind or startling pedestrians in the process.

Be extra cautious of hidden areas around the crossings such as overgrown vegetation or parked vehicles that can obscure your view and hide you from people wanting to cross, also being mindful of disabled, older and young pedestrians, as they may be more vulnerable or require more time to cross.

But with careful speed reduction with great timing you should always be prepared to stop safely when required.

The five main types again are:

- Pelican
- Zebra
- Toucan
- Equestrian/Pegasus
- Puffin

You will find your overall drive will be a lot smoother and less stressful if you adopt this technique and making driving a far more enjoyable ride for your passengers too.

25) POSITIONING

Normal stops: When planning to stop there are multiple things to take into consideration, such as, stopping in a safe legal and convenient place ensuring not causing a hazard, danger or in a place that's not an inconvenience to others. Stay close to the kerb without scraping it is also important, because traffic behind may think you're stuck in traffic and may not have planned to overtake you, after all, your position is a signal.

THE TEST

TIP: When asked to pull up on the left or right, make sure you check your main mirror followed by the directional mirror in the direction you intend to go and physically act on what you see, ie: if no one is present then there's no need to signal! Do things as a conscious decision, not based on routine.

Watch out for entrances, driveways, bus stops, corners, dead ground, peak of hills, road markings that prohibit access, etc. Also make sure you stop or pause at the end of roads correctly, not five yards short or five yards over the end of the road. Pay attention to exactly where the end of the road is!

26) AWARENESS AND PLANNING

In my mind this is probably the biggest area of concern and makes the driver either a good driver or a bad one. As an instructor and seeing thousands of tests experience tells me it all boils down to this section. When you look at a test sheet and see faults in almost any category, if you psycho-analyse the driving faults they very often bounce back to this section, let me explain: the DVSA say in a roundabout way that under this heading drivers must be aware of road users at all times!

You must plan and know the intention of all road users, predict what they are going to do and act in advance and react in good time. Considering the road weather and traffic conditions as well as vulnerable road users, such as pedestrians, motorbikes, horse riders, etc...

So, if you drove too fast, you wouldn't be able to respond quick enough compared with driving slower thus reducing the risk even though you were under the speed limit. Or if you got marked down for clearance of obstructions, had you planned ahead and moved out earlier this wouldn't be a issue or lets say use of mirrors was lacking, if you had slowed down and had more time you wouldn't have missed your mirror checks you would have had time for your hazard drill (MSM/PSGL routine)

So, in short, I always run at least 3 mock tests to see where the faults lie and go back to the awareness and planning. Pupils often agree: if they adopted awareness and planning, the more the overall faults drop like flies.

27) ANCILLARY CONTROLS

Whilst on the move the examiner will ask you to use a secondary control such as opening a window or switch on lights/fog lights/full beam, demisters or operate the horn, etc, without loss of control of the car, slowing down or swerving, you must be in full control of the car and be comfortable in making any adjustments.

Now this isn't just for test, remember once you've passed the test and get in your own car, please before you go anywhere, find out where everything is. People do crash when they get distracted, become familiar straight away, there are no excuses.

Now just a few more pointers, with regards to eco-driving, think about how your driving attitude effects the atmosphere, drive in a friendly manner, plan well ahead, switch the engine off when waiting for a while such as bridge going up or level crossings, etc, use gentle acceleration, avoid revving the engine or having to brake sharply. You must also declare any change to your health since you last applied for your licence. If there have been any changes, inform the authorities as it's a criminal offence to make a false statement to obtain a licence and you could be prosecuted.

Funny stories

Just to lighten the mood of my book I would like to share some funny stories with you all. I won't use the names of my top five tribulations but I know they all know who they are and may giggle out loud when they see these stories written.

 The first story is of a young lady that by all standards was a great driver, her only downfall in driving was the ability to use her brain.

So, the lesson on this occasion was to pull over and park the car in a safe convenient and legal place. Once I said park up she forgot to check her mirrors, so off we go again!

Pull up and she checked mirrors but didn't give a signal when required.
Pull up, checked mirrors and signalled but not necessary on this occasion.
Pull up, wasn't parked in a legal place
Pull up, wasn't in a safe place
Pull up, didn't check mirrors or signal so we were going around in circles, she knew exactly what to do she knew without exception why, but for some reason after nearly one and a half hours she just couldn't get it right, feeling a little low I had a great idea I would take her down a road that was straight, no road markings, no traffic, no signposts no NOTHING so all she would have to do is basically stop.

How hard could that be?.... I was already getting ready to praise her, until I said the magic words "I would like you to park up in a safe, legal and convenient place. She checked her mirrors, she considered a signal, she slowed down beautifully and turned left into somebody's garden and parked on their lawn at 9:30 pm!

WOW I never saw that coming.... The bedroom lights came on and after I had controlled my laughter and moved off the premises, I had to ask WHY?

The answer she gave was "everyone else has parked on their drives I honestly thought it was a safe, legal and convenient place to be". Oblivious to the fact that the road I had chosen was all the above, she saw the funny side of what she had done, and since then all was good!

 My next funny story was let's say a bit of a sore subject!

Whilst completing an intensive course over 5 days my pupil came from a very respectful upbringing and very modest home, she had fine manners and projected herself very well indeed. Until late one afternoon on her first day, out in the sticks, she required a lavatory. As you can imagine there wasn't such luxury bathrooms available so she used the hedge, okay that seems reasonable enough, after all when you got to go, you've got to go right!

She climbed over a gate in a field and disappeared, after about 1 minute I heard a shriek then a scream, naturally I called out to ask if everything was okay, no response? So, I hailed her again and a weeping voice cried no, no I'm not okay.

I informed her I was coming to her rescue only to find this very beautiful young lady was …. well…. completely naked from the bottom downwards bent over exposing her …. rear end! Look she said look… …a little gingerly I had a closer inspection not wishing to embarrass her to find 2 bad red lines across her perfectly formed bottom where she had squatted on the electric fence that kept the horses in, along with a few stinging nettles around some very sensitive body parts.

I explained there was nothing to worry about and assured her the pain would go by the next day and arranged a little cushion for her for when she got back in the car. Little did she know I wasn't that sympathetic and was crying with laughter inside, but felt I managed to be professional even in this time of need.

Golden rule ladies, look before you squat and if something goes wrong don't tell your instructor, you may end up in a book!!

Now this is a great story, using client-centred learning, where I ask a question and try to extract the answer from my pupil.

This normally works well, even if the pupil doesn't understand the question, I can usually ask another, which most people would then see where I was going with it.

Not this time and not with this pupil!

The question was "why would you want to only circulate the air inside the car as opposed to bringing the outside air into the car?"

My pupil went quiet, looked at the air controls, thought hard and said "to stop fog coming in"

So naturally I said "hmmm, okay why" well she said if too much fog comes in I won't be able to see!

I then said "I guess that could be a problem, especially if it starts raining in the car!"

I then said what would you do in this situation then?

"Open my window" she replied.

At this point my giggles started….so I said wont it be raining outside as well then? She looked a little confused now, so I put her mind on hold and suggested, that perhaps the car wouldn't suck fog in, and it certainly wouldn't rain inside the car, but it was to stop pollution entering the car such as carbon monoxide, smoke pollen etc…. but fog mist clouds and rainbows wouldn't have been a real concern.

She saw the funny side of her suggestions, which I'm for her sake very pleased about.

FUNNY STORIES

4. Having fun in the car with pupils is great it puts their mind at ease and I think if you're happy you do learn far quicker, however sometimes it doesn't always work out like that. I was teaching a dear friend of mine to drive back in the late 90's. Something tickled us both at the start of the lesson and we both had laughs that were contagious, my friend started hyperventilating which made us both laugh even more, I had a brown bag which she breathed into but neither of us stopped laughing, I mean I was belly laughing and crying, tears rolling down my cheeks.

Her brown bag was going in and out a million miles per hour! 47 minutes later we managed to regain calmness and had to arrange another lesson, as I could not attempt to charge her for that hour which in turn set us both off again!!!

As you can imagine coaching so many people over all these years you meet so many characters, from doctors to drug dealers.

For me I always treated each person as an equal, achieving their goal together, never judged them, or shown anything other than the job in hand. I have picked pupils up drove them to the police station to have them breathalysed after suspecting them of being over the limit, then left them there as I was normally right.

Sent pupils back to their house to put clothes on suitable for lessons so I didn't feel so uncomfortable with them in the car. Had words with affluent parents about why I require payment at the start of lessons not 2 months down the line, as I had bills to pay too.

But overall over the last 2 decades I have met and trained some great people and to be part of their journey means so much to me.

5. **Which leads me to my next story**, a pupil I'm still coaching today, this isn't that funny but deserves a mention, over the last 6 years this very anxious lady entered my world of tuition.

To give a little background she was about 45 with no real hand-eye coordination, she suffered panic attacks every time before she drove.

Having only a hour a week due to hard times she really wanted this, but never believed she could ever drive, I said we would take her at her own pace, I promised I would never push her, we started at about 5 mph of which seemed too fast for her, with screaming, swearing, shouting, freezing up you name it, she was petrified, I promised her I would never give up on her and each week praised her when required, having celebrated each little mile stone we reached with praise.

It took a good 20 weeks just to get her to turn left and right into roads where most pupils would be booking their practical tests by now, but she was making progress, she was worried about upsetting other drivers, and to be perfectly honest made me doubt my ability to ever get her to test standard on many occasions. But I wasn't going to give up on her and she was determined to pass.

After about 4 years, finally things started to fall into place, her cognitive thinking was much better, she had started to show signs that her judgement and observation and forward planning was coming together, but then her mother turned ill and she requested a break for a while, no problem...

During this break I transferred to west Yorkshire with wife and family as wife gained a wonderful opportunity for work, it was only for a year and then came back, starting my business back up in Suffolk I contacted this lady again to see if she was ready to continue, she agreed and on our first meeting she informed me her life had been a real mess, her mother had sadly passed away, she had fallen out with her sister and swore she would never speak to her again. To top it off had been mentally unwell, suffering from being an alcoholic and suicidal, in a complete cycle of depression.

But now she was to start driving again, it gave her the motivation to seek help with the drinking. She soon gained self-esteem and within a few weeks she was back, just as she had left off, I revised my coaching pattern, started making her be more responsible for her actions, having chats in the car about life and encouraged and supported ideas she was having and in over a year became a completely different person, totally off the alcohol. Secured a voluntary job helping those with issues, getting involved in local support projects, finding her own independence and gaining confidence. Her driving was getting much better so I kept pushing her to make progress and finally encouraged her to go for her test, she booked it!

Now to get this far was already a massive achievement and so we went and did the test, and even though she failed I was so proud of her for completing it, she had never driven with anybody else and only failed with 1 serious fault which in hindsight she could have so easily avoided, so her confidence wasn't shaken and for the first time in her life she now believes the test is do-able.

I commend her for her attitude, she has her next test very soon, and if she fails it again I know despite being a little upset she will go back and she will always give it her all, and not long from now she will be triumphant and I will be so emotional when this day comes because I understand everything she has been through, every barrier anyone could experience, this lady has had.

Just hope she doesn't jam her hair in the door and try to look over her left shoulder again! That was an experience.

PS: Teresa has finally passed 3rd time lucky, with no more than a handful of minors!

FUNNY STORIES

 The man with the bushy beard – this is a story that caused karma when laughing at someone else's misfortune.

I was teaching a pupil call Danni, a friend of my family, I had taught her mother some 18 years earlier and we had lots of laughter and normally ended in fits of giggles and found it nearly impossible to focus or give a quality lesson, but I hadn't had the opportunity to know Danni very well, so humour had been replaced with serious lessons.

On this particular day we drove along a road on the outskirts of Lowestoft towards a village called Corton.

At the end of this read was a top sign, so Danni pauses at the end and applied the handbrake. On looking to the right we both saw a man in his early 20's with a big busy beard riding his bike. He was blocking our vision so we stayed paused as it appeared that he was stopping and was going to proceed through a gate. As his bike stopped he multi-tasked putting his left foot down onto the kerb whilst unlocking the gate. All should have been well except his foot missed the kerb as the gate opened and in slow motion he disappeared straight into the garden just like Del Boy going through the Nags Head bar.

Well that was it, we looked at each other and burst out laughing. With the windows open the roar of laughter escalated to an almost uncontrollable bladder malfunction whilst at the same time thinking we should get out to help this poor lad whilst allowing time to compose ourselves. However, he suddenly popped back up brushing leaves off himself only to engage his eyes on a learner car holding up traffic in complete belly laughter. He recognized we were laughing at him and in the momentary lapse of reasoning and the sound of infectious chuckles he started laughing as well. His shoulders were bouncing up and down like the honey monster and belly too! That was it, no Danni and I looked at each other again and couldn't see through the tears. Danni then began to hyperventilate which made it even funnier and we were both incapacitated through laughter. Cars started honking but the three of us were just a mess.

PS: Danni went on to pass her practical test with only 5 minors.

I soon composed myself enough to move the car out of the way but had to pull up shortly after to allow ourselves to calm down and get it out of our systems. I did feel bad for holding the traffic up and felt sorry for the man with the bushy beard, but it was the situation we found funny, not anything about him as a person.

I did have the privilege of seeing this man once again approximately 3 weeks later whilst I was going to pick the same pupil up. He lent his bike against a shop wall but as he walked away his bag caught his handle bars and the bike fell over again. Well that was me done in again for 2 minutes and a further 15 minutes after I told Danni.

So I have currently put my prices down for people with bushy beards as whoever this person is he need to come to me for driving lessons as I am sure it could not go any worse than his biking had.

The COVID-19 guessing game

December 2020 and due to COVID-19 it's not unusual for pupils and instructors to wear masks.

I was taking a client called Harvey for a 2 hour lesson as he had his test booked and his parents had been training him, I have only met him a couple of times in the past but due to lockdown some months have past.

I'm waiting at the train station as he has to travel some 30 miles to get to me. He turns up in his mums car, says goodbye to his mother and jumps in, great we are all good to go.

So part of my due diligence I open my folder look at his records to familiarise myself with his progress, take his temperature and then have a conversation with him about what he has done and what we need to do next! We sat in the car for a good 15 minutes and he agreed with my previous observations and fault analysis.

I asked if he had any questions and he replied "yes I do have one" go ahead I encouraged, "why do you keep calling me Harvey my names Harry"? I said no it's Harvey and he assured me he knew his own name!

I asked what his father's name was and he told me! And then the penny dropped, He had a new driving instructor of which he had never met and thought I was him and I didn't recognise him due to the masks!

With that Harvey banged on my window and this guys driving instructor then turned up!

Imagine if he never asked that important question, we would have been off down the dual carriageway leaving my poor pupil in the cold and a very grumpy instructor in a car park on his lonesome.

I did joke and say I can't believe you got into a car with a stranger. We laughed as this situation confused both of us and has never happened in my 25 years of teaching! Mutual embarrassment, can't beat it.

Beccles Tyre Centre

Tyres, puncture repairs, batteries, exhausts, brakes, suspension, wheel alignment, servicing and repairs

Tel: 01502 712113
Unit 9 Tilia Court, Worlingham, Beccles, Suffolk, NR34 7BF

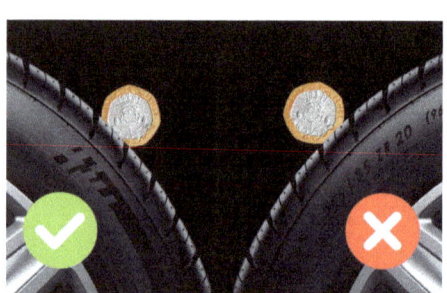
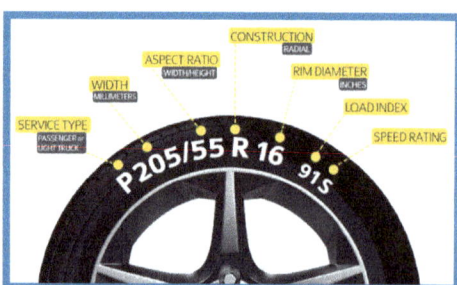
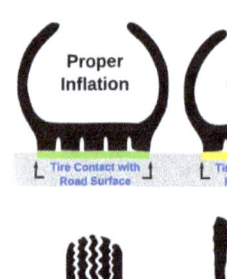  
 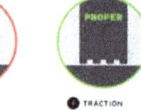 

Juler Tooke is proud to be a sponsor of HELP, DON'T HINDER

Helping your business grow

At Juler Tooke we aim to help our clients attain their goals through the provision of expertise and a range of services that supports them in all of their financial endeavours.

Established in 1974, Juler Tooke Accountants rapidly developed a reputation for providing expert advice based on sound principals together with a clear understanding of clients' requirements delivered in a friendly and efficient manner.

www.julertooke.co.uk

Please feel free to contact us with any enquires.
Call: 01502 516861 or email: info@julertooke.co.uk

Lothing House, 7 Quay View Business Park, Barnards Way, Lowestoft, Suffolk NR32 2HD

WITH GRATEFUL THANKS

With Grateful Thanks

I would like to take this final opportunity to thank everyone who has purchased this book and added support to these two excellent charities 'EAAA & BRAKE' as well as everyone who has helped me to write this book, all my past and present pupils and everyone who has been part of this successful journey.

Hopefully you enjoyed it and learnt something of value. As well as the many people who will benefit in the future, I would also like to dedicate this book in loving memory to Harley George Snowling, a great pupil I really enjoyed teaching, who not just made me and Nan proud but all his family and friends too with his epic first time pass.

HELP – DON'T HINDER

WITH GRATEFUL THANKS

HELP – DON'T HINDER

WITH GRATEFUL THANKS

WITH GRATEFUL THANKS

WITH GRATEFUL THANKS

Covid 2020-2021 Rules and restrictions commence – using PPE and carrying out due diligence for essential key workers

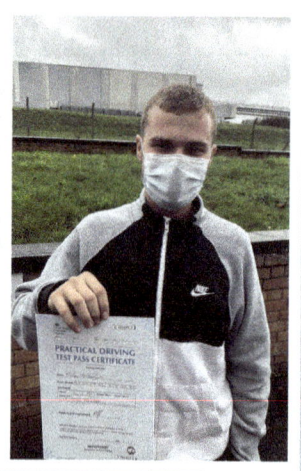
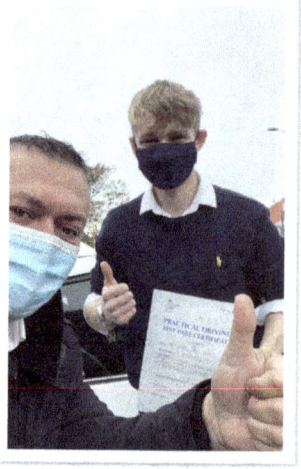
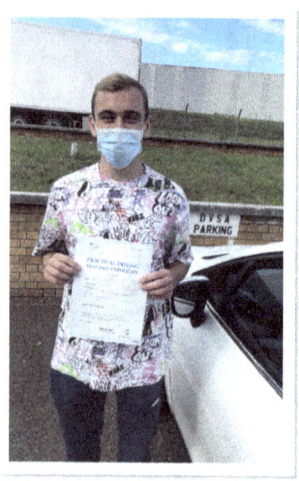
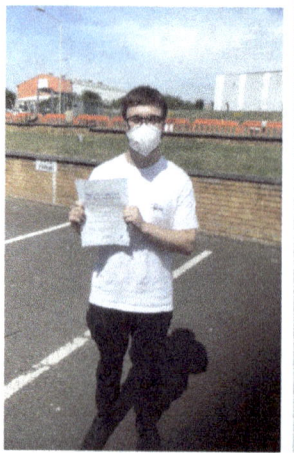

WITH GRATEFUL THANKS

Not forgetting Miss Kylie Thompson AKA: Dory.

WITH GRATEFUL THANKS

And many thousands more!

WITH GRATEFUL THANKS

HELP – DON'T HINDER

ACKNOWLEDGEMENTS

Acknowledgements

I would like to thank and show acknowledgment to all the businesses that have supported myself and my driving school over the last 25 years by going above and beyond their normal requirements as each company in my eyes have been nothing less than exceptional and I have absolute confidence in recommending them for the highest standards in their fields of expertise, customer care, service and after care.

HOLDEN GROUP
22 Heigham St, Norwich NR2 4TF
01603 664411

For new and used quality cars at fantastic deals and after care service, I have now used for over 10 years for business and personal cars, and even my pupils have benefited from being introduced to this family run company owned by Mr Tim Holden. I have had the pleasure from doing my business with Mr Dariusz Wlodarczyk who has been absolutely amazing in every area, just one of the many staff here that relentlessly go above and beyond any situation and constantly make every sale a totally stress-free and relaxed experience.

BECCLES TYRE CENTRE
Tilia Ct Beccles Suffolk NR34 7BF
01502 712113

I have used this company for 5 years now for all my tyres, batteries and exhausts. Andy and his team have proved I'm a valued customer, their prices and service – always with a smile – has been outstanding.

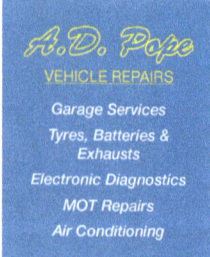

AD POPE
10-18 Pinbush Rd South Lowestoft Ind. Est. Lowestoft NR33 7NL
01502 584466

Adrian and his team of fine mechanics have gone above and beyond each and every time I've needed a service or help over the last 25 years, nothing has ever been too much and they have accommodated me every time, getting my car back on the road quickly and cost effectively.

HELP – DON'T HINDER

ACKNOWLEDGEMENTS

Furthermore...

I would like to say a very special thank you to my family for their continued love and support, not just in the making of this book, but in everything I have done. Thank you Mary, Emma and Toby Ritchie.

I would also like to thank my mother Margaret and father David Ritchie for their inputs.

And last, but by no means least, I would like to thank an individual who was instrumental in me finishing this book. Without him, it would have been impossible and I can not thank him enough for his help and guidance. You know who you are!

www.ingramcontent.com/pod-product-compliance
Lightning Source LLC
Chambersburg PA
CBHW050440010526
44118CB00013B/1617